W9-BVU-728

CASS LIBRARY OF AFRICAN STUDIES

GENERAL STUDIES

No. 54

Editorial Adviser: JOHN RALPH WILLIS

An 1890 Pioneer
(The late Arthur Eyre)

OLD
RHODESIAN DAYS

HUGH MARSHALL HOLE

FRANK CASS & CO. LTD.
1968

Published by
FRANK CASS AND COMPANY LIMITED
67 Great Russell Street, London WC1
by arrangement with Macmillan and Co. Ltd.

| First edition | 1928 |
| New impression | 1968 |

Printed in Holland by
N.V. Grafische Industrie Haarlem

CONTENTS

LIST OF ILLUSTRATIONS

INTRODUCTION.

In these pages I have endeavoured to recapture a little of the atmosphere which surrounded the early settlers of Rhodesia.

To the present generation with their railways, their motor-cars and their wireless telegraphy the more leisurely existence of the bullock-waggon days may appear dull, but it had its charm and was not without occasional excitement. It provided opportunities for the development of character—national as well as individual, and it was constantly relieved by the exhilarating sense of participation in a great adventure.

I dedicate
these sketches to the
surviving Pioneers
of
Mashonaland and Matabeleland

Sa ku bona zonki

OLD RHODESIAN DAYS

CHAPTER I.

TWILIGHT.

HAVE you noticed that Africa is seldom called " The Dark Continent " nowadays ?

Until late in the last century it was commonly so spoken of, and fully justified the name. To the great body of Englishmen it then meant little more than an outline on the map. As to what lay behind no one troubled much. A certain flutter of interest was excited by Livingstone's travels and by his revelations of the horrors of the slave trade, but, except in missionary circles, that soon languished. Hammer-blows were needed to break through the apathy with which, in the mid-Victorian period, our race habitually regarded distant countries and peoples, and, so far as Africa was concerned, it was not until 1879 that such blows began to fall. Then, in quick succession, we had the Zulu war, the Basuto revolt, and the first Boer War. A little later British impassiveness was stirred by Stanley's much-advertised mission for the relief of Emin Pasha, and by the tragic climax of Gordon's lonely vigil at Khartoum.

Simultaneously, out of the wilderness, arose a prophet. An obscure official in Natal began to write novels about things he had seen—but mostly dreamed ; half-forgotten legends of hidden treasure of gold and ivory ; of ancient peoples and ruined cities in the secret recesses of the unknown interior. " King Solomon's Mines ; " " The Witch's Head " ; " Allan Quatermain " ! The very names revive the tingle of schoolboy curiosity.

The books fell upon fruitful soil ; for in those days there was a good deal of restlessness in the Homeland. The steady increase of population in the prosperous Victorian era was beginning to squeeze the middle classes ; parents were beginning to look abroad for openings for their sons ; sons were fretting at the monotony of mediocre posts in offices and warehouses.

History is made by the right man seizing the ripe moment. At the very time when these influences were at work there came into the open an Englishman who had for years been brooding over schemes for increasing his country's ascendancy in Africa, and had now acquired sufficient financial and political weight to set the wheels in motion.

This was Cecil Rhodes.

Far beyond the narrow confines of the Cape Colony, the Transvaal and Natal he saw an immense region, sparsely populated by fierce and barbarous black men. The Portuguese explorers of the 16th century called it " Monomotapa," and it had long been associated with reports of gold mines of fabulous richness, and of unknown races who had built elaborate temples and forts of hewn stone and then disappeared. Inspired, perhaps, by Rider Haggard some were convinced that these were the relics of the miners who dug the gold for Balkis, Queen of Sheba, and that Monomotapa was actually the Land of Ophir. The few hunters and traders who had reached these parts brought back fascinating tales of the prodigious herds of elephants, camelopards and other beasts that roamed in the forests of the Zambesi, and related hair-raising escapes from lions and wounded buffaloes. Some shewed fragments of rock studded with visible gold, and all spoke impressively of the Matabele, the Angoni, and other ferocious tribes that lived by rapine and slaughter.

So when Rhodes began coolly to talk about sending up an expedition to occupy this region of thrilling possibilities, and when, simultaneously, Boers, Belgians, Portuguese and Germans were seen to be casting avaricious glances in the same direction, a wave of enthusiasm seized upon young Englishmen at home and in the South African colonies, and a keen competition to take part in the enterprise.

Rhodes had for some years made his headquarters at Kimberley, the centre of the diamond industry, in Griqualand West. As the terminus of the Cape railway system it was the jumping-off ground for the newly-discovered gold-fields of Witwatersrand, and the focus of most of the speculative activity of South Africa. Here, in '88, Rhodes achieved the final amalgamation of the various diamond companies, and here in the following year he matured his plans for the conquest of the North.

In that year it was my great good fortune to arrive in Kimberley, a raw youngster from England. It was the very eve of the granting of the Royal Charter which gave Rhodes the right to carry the Union Jack into the remote interior.

In order to have all arrangements immediately under his eye he opened a small office at Kimberley and gave me a post

The Kimberley Mine in 1889

in it, so that I was actively concerned in the preparations for the despatch of the Pioneer expedition to Mashonaland and of the less public, but equally important missions to Barotseland, Angoniland and other native kingdoms. I was also thrown into daily contact with Jameson, Maguire, Colquhoun, Selous and other leading actors in the drama which was to follow, and a little later I myself was privileged to take part in the Northward movement and in the settlement of what is now Rhodesia. The political history of those days I have dealt with elsewhere,* but there were casual incidents—strange, humorous and pathetic—which, though unimportant historically, gave colour and distinctiveness to the undertaking, and shed light on the characters of those engaged in it. It is of this side of the Pioneer days of Rhodesia that I propose to speak in the present volume.

Kimberley in '89 was the hub of South Africa. But after a tedious rail journey of thirty-six hours from Capetown across the dusty waste of the Karroo desert its first appearance was to me singularly unimpressive. A confused mass of galvanised iron shanties, flung higgledy-piggledy over a treeless expanse of barren veld ; a few drab buildings of brick and stone ; here and there the head gear of a mine, and everywhere the tailing-heaps of " blue ground " which had been hauled up from the bowels of the earth and spread, like a great grey blanket, over the whole landscape—this was what I saw, and I found little encouragement to hope for entertainment from the listless sun-burnt faces of the few rather battered white men who were abroad in the early morning of my arrival.

During the short drive across the market square to the hotel I gazed with curiosity on the clumsy Boer waggons, piled high with firewood and other produce, assembling for the regular morning market. The air echoed to the strident yells of the native drivers and the crack of their long whips, beneath which one could hear the heavy breathing of the long teams of oxen now preparing to lie down in the yoke and chew placidly, until the business of their masters should be at an end.

Suddenly there was a hubbub in one of the side streets, out of which darted the figure of a stark naked European daubed with tar, to which adhered a few inadequate feathers. He was flying as if for his life, and in a twinkling disappeared on the far side of the square, pursued by a howling mob of rough-looking white men, Cape boys, and even one or two women.

---

* " The Making of Rhodesia," pub. 1926.

As this was my first glimpse of the social side of a mining town, I at first thought that what I had seen was an ordinary every-day event, to which in time I should get accustomed. Later I learnt that the victim had been paying unwelcome attentions to the wife of a neighbour, who had decided to deal with the matter summarily, and that the subsequent proceedings were sufficiently unusual to merit a whole column in the daily " Advertiser."

But although nothing quite so sensational occurred during the eighteen months I spent on the " Fields," the life was far from monotonous. The first Witwatersrand gold boom was beginning to wane, but nevertheless the streets around the diamond market were often crowded with a dense mob of excited brokers and speculators shouting prices as bookies do the odds ; and after business hours the same crowd gathered at the bars of the principal hotels and washed down the day's transactions in copious draughts of champagne and whiskey.

Diamond shares had a limited market, for most of the mines had by then been amalgamated ; but diamonds themselves were bought and sold openly and legitimately by licensed dealers, and secretly and illicitly by a series of crooks, ranging from men (and women) moving in respectable circles down to the lowest Cape boy, who acted as a fence for thievish natives employed on the mines.   In spite of the special laws for putting down the latter traffic, and of the Draconian penalties exacted against offenders (sentences of three or four years' hard labour on the Capetown breakwater were by no means uncommon, even for Europeans), the profits were so enormous and the risk of detection apparently so slight that the crime of illicit diamond buying—more familiarly " I.D.B."—was still prevalent when I first knew the " Fields." Honest men were haunted by an uneasy fear lest, from associating unawares with someone marked by the police, they might themselves incur suspicion. The mere possession of an uncut diamond was a serious crime, punishable by a term of imprisonment. I once picked up a small stone in the street after a rain storm, and so great was my dread of being seen with it that I literally ran to the police station to report and hand it over, receiving for my honesty a few shillings commission.

Many were the stories current of the ingenuity displayed by amateur or habitual offenders in concealing and disposing of their illicit stones.   The following case, in which the principal actor was a young man mixing in my own set, I do not remember to have seen in print.

In the sorting office of one of the mining companies it was

the practice to hand the diamonds received from the mine—
the daily " wash-up " as it was called—to two clerks, whose
duty it was to take them to the laboratory for a bath in some
strong acid—nitric, I suppose—for the purpose of removing
any small particles of sand or dirt which might be adhering to
them. Each parcel of stones was weighed carefully before
and after this process, but the weight lost in the acid bath was
a variable quantity. In a parcel of a hundred carats, for
instance, the difference might be only half a carat, or it might
be over a carat. C——, a smart clerk employed on this duty,
took advantage of this uncertain factor. When his colleague's
back was turned he purloined the smallest stone he could see
in the parcel—perhaps a half-carat diamond. The loss was
too insignificant to attract attention when the parcel was re-
weighed. When the next lot was handed to him he added to
it this small stone and took out one a little bigger, and so went
on with each successive parcel, always exchanging the stone in
his possession for one a trifle larger, until he had secured a
diamond of two or three carats. This he kept. Then he began
again, as before, with a very small stone.

From what followed it was clear that C—— had been
playing this little game for some months and had accumulated
a respectable hoard of medium-sized stones, and he might have
gone on indefinitely had not an accident revealed the trick.
He shared lodgings with a friend employed at one of the local
banks, who came under suspicion for some defalcation wholly
unconnected with diamonds. The lodgings were searched by
the police in their absence and in the common sitting-room a
little packet of about twenty diamonds was found concealed
behind a picture. A watch was set and eventually C—— was
caught with the bag in his hands. He then confessed the whole
business. His age was taken into consideration, but nevertheless
he served a term on the breakwater.

In the general atmosphere of suspicion sinister rumours
used to circulate round anyone who made money with
conspicuous rapidity, and, in fact, the fortunes of several of
the most successful speculators were said to be tainted. When
individual holdings were still being worked on the Kimberley
mine the ownership of a claim and a digger's licence were all
that was required to account for the legitimate possession of
rough diamonds. It was well known that much of the ground
on the edge of the mine was barren, but in intelligent hands it
could be turned to account. A certain needy speculator who
afterwards became immensely wealthy bought an outside claim

for a mere song. Under cover of night he would from time to time stealthily tip into it a handful of stones obtained cheaply from Kafirs, fences, or other crooks. By day he would assiduously work the claim, regardless of the jeers of those who knew it was worthless, but when diamonds were produced from it with unfailing regularity, and especially when among them were stones recognisable as having come from the river diggings twenty miles off (for experts could always tell a river stone from a mined one), their derision was turned into admiration. This little dodge attracted imitators, and the authorities soon found means to cope with the practice, but its inventor's fortune was made.

The amalgamation of the diamond companies led to the introduction of the " Compound " system whereby native employees were kept prisoners during their engagement and, as they often secreted stones by swallowing them, for a few days after their time was up. The facilities for I.D.B. were now immensely reduced, though ingenious natives still found means to evade the vigilance of the overseers, and to convey diamonds from the mines to the outer world. The diamondiferous clay when first brought to the surface was spread on " floors," where it was left for some time exposed to the decomposing action of the weather, and was constantly turned over by gangs of natives. The floors were separated from the public thoroughfares by high fences of barbed wire. One day a party of time-expired natives, proceeding along one of the roads, began to hurl insults at a gang of workers engaged inside and not very far from the fence. High words were exchanged and then some stones were thrown by the outside party, whereat a member of the working gang was so provoked that he seized a clod of clay and flung it at a native in the road, who promptly picked it up and put it in his pocket. He was marked and arrested, when the lump of clay was found to contain a large and valuable white diamond.

CHAPTER II.

UP-COUNTRY.

THERE'S magic in these words for all old South Africans.

Just as phrases coined in the Great War—"Over the top," "Blighty," and the like—will always stir some memory in those who once used them in their daily talk, so "Up-country" will bring back to the Pioneer of the 'nineties a recollection of the creaking waggon; the patient, straining bullocks; the unearthly scream of a hyæna breaking in on the soft silence of the veld at night; the camp fire at the outspan, and the cool, early trek when the morning star is paling before the grey-green dawn. His pulse will beat faster at the thought of his first glimpse of a sable antelope; he will lick his lips as his mind goes back to the guinea-fowl stew earned on the road by his own gun. Only the pleasant experiences are remembered. The discomforts are forgotten, or merely recalled with a grin.

When I first reached the diamond fields, "up-country" still meant Mafeking and Bechuanaland. Bulawayo was the "far north," and all that lay beyond the Zambesi River was the unknown interior. True, we heard of men—sometimes actually saw them—who had penetrated to these remote places, and even written books about them; but that I or any of my friends then earning a monthly pittance at de Beers, or in a share-broker's office, or in one of the banks, should soon be familiar with the distant wilds where Livingstone trod his solitary path, where his successors, Helm and Coillard, laboured unfruitfully to teach Christ to savages, and where Selous galloped after giraffe and antelope, would have seemed incredible, and even ridiculous. And yet the time was fast approaching when most of us were to have a share in the great adventure the scheme of which was already maturing in Rhodes' brain.

Among minor excitements in those days were the arrivals and departures of Gibson's coaches, which plied between Kimberley and the new-born city of gold—Johannesburg— carrying mails and passengers. These lumbering vehicles were usually drawn by ten mules with a pair of horses as leaders. Very smart and fresh were the teams and the passengers starting for the first stage northwards; very dirty and bedraggled were the latter on arrival after three days' bumping along the so-called roads.   But how we envied them !   How bronzed and vigorous was their appearance !   What tales they had to tell of fortunes made on the Reef ; and how flush they were of cash—at first, till the slump came ; and then we all blessed our stars that we had stuck to humdrum Kimberley.

It would be difficult to conceive a more odious and uncomfortable means of travel than these mail coaches, of which in after years I had ample experience.   Day and night there was no rest, save a short halt at each stage while fresh teams were being inspanned, and for half-an-hour at irregular intervals for a hasty meal—called by courtesy breakfast or dinner—at some wayside store.   Nine travellers were boxed up inside a space about big enough for four, while several others were balanced precariously on the mail-bags heaped on the roof, to which prudent ones usually strapped themselves for fear of being overcome by drowsiness and shot off by a sudden jolt.   With the shaking and bumping, you would at first think any chance of sleep impossible, but from sheer exhaustion you generally dosed off sooner or later, with your head on your neighbour's shoulder, for all formality broke down under the stress of the common misery.

The reins were held by a coloured boy, and the immense whip, with a lash long enough to tickle up the leaders, was wielded by a white man, called, oddly enough, the " Driver."   Both were expert at guiding the team over awkward bits of road, and upsets were comparatively rare.   Occasionally, however, a boulder or broken place in the track caused a capsize.   The unhappy passengers inside were thrown into a helpless, struggling heap, while those on the roof came tumbling off in confusion, accompanied by the mailbags and luggage.   There comes to my memory an accident of this kind when the coach turned turtle.   One of the inside passengers was a lively Frenchwoman, and when the crash came she found herself in the embarrassing position of being pinned down by the body of a stout stockbroker, who was literally sitting on her face.   The latter instantly struggled to his feet with a yell of pain, but attention was turned mainly to the lady.   " Did he hurt you ? " asked one sympathiser.   " Non, non ! " she replied.   " I bite 'eem ! "

Once a week a far less pretentious equipage started for Vryburg, Mafeking and Khama's country.   This was a " Cape cart " carrying Her Majesty's mails and two or three passengers—usually police officers travelling on duty or prosperous traders returning to their stores in Bechuanaland.   Humbler folk went by bullock waggon, which didn't mean that they sat inside and smoked, but merely that they were allowed to put their provisions and kit on the vehicle, to sleep under it when it was outspanned, and to walk alongside when it trekked at the habitual snail-like rate of two miles an hour.

At Kimberley, one afternoon in November, 1889, a group of young Englishmen clustered round a heavily-loaded ox-waggon outside the warehouse of Messrs. Hill and Paddon, general dealers and produce merchants. Twelve of them were distinguished by wearing new corduroy breeches, and flannel shirts, open at the neck and with rolled-up sleeves. These were obviously starting on a journey and the rest were seeing them off. Where were they going ? They would have been puzzled to explain, but all knew that Mr. Rhodes had some expedition in view—something to do with King Lobengula, and Mashonaland, and gold-reefs. He had given them each ten pounds and an outfit, and told them he wanted them to go to Mafeking and there await further orders. They thought they might get some shooting, and possibly even some fighting with the Matabele or other aggressive tribes up North. At any rate all felt the vague thrill of adventures to come.

These young men were afterwards known as "Rhodes' Apostles." Hitherto they had mostly been working in offices at Kimberley or Capetown, or in the de Beers compound. Now their chance had come and almost all of them were destined to make their mark in the years to come. One of them—Pat Campbell—the youthful husband of a lady then making her début on the English stage—was to fall in action ten years later in the Boer War ; another was Bob Coryndon, who lived to be the Governor of Kenya and other African Colonies. A third was Johnny Grimmer, afterwards the intimate friend and secretary of Rhodes himself. To-day two or three only survive and if they happen on these words they will admit, I think, that their real life began on that November afternoon outside Hill and Paddon's store.

As a matter of fact Rhodes himself had no very definite plans for them, for the pioneer column, which afterwards marched into Mashonaland, did not take shape till months afterwards. But he had a general idea of sending as many young British Colonials as possible into the country covered by his Charter, and this little party was intended to be—as indeed it actually became—the advance guard of an army of settlers.

Simultaneously with their departure, and just as inconspicuously, another party started, on the outskirts of Kimberley, cutting the first sods of the earthworks for the new line which was ultimately to become the great Rhodesian Railway system —reaching northwards to the Congo Free State and across the continent from Bulawayo to the Indian Ocean.

Less than a fortnight had elapsed since the Charter had been signed in London, and Rhodes was already at work blazing the trail.

Before the rails reached Vryburg the pioneer column had completed its historic march to Mashonaland and had built a fort on the site of the modern town of Salisbury. After them through the awful wet season of 1890-91 there crawled a thin stream of prospectors, speculators, traders and the like, struggling painfully with bullock transport to reach the promised land of gold. They got there—most of them—after a weary and heart-breaking journey of a thousand miles through Bechuanaland and Southern Matabeleland, but on the banks of the swollen rivers where they lay rotting, sometimes for weeks, they left many little piles of stones to mark the last resting place of companions whom fever and privation had claimed as victims.

During that wet season communication with the South was only maintained by means of relays of mounted despatch riders, and even this method was unavailing in January and February when the rivers became impassable. The result was that all sorts of baseless rumours gained credence as to events in the newly-occupied territory. Monty Bowden, who before joining the pioneer force had been a well-known and popular member of an English County cricket team, was one of several whose death was reported and cabled to his relatives at home. But he was by no means dead, and afterwards took a morbid pleasure in reading his own obituary notices and especially the accounts of a memorial service in his native county. An even stranger experience befell Colonel Pennefather, the Commander of the Police. He had gone down the line on some duty or other and was cut off by flooded rivers from returning. At one of the largest rivers—the Lundi—two despatch riders, unable to cross, hailed each other from opposite banks. " Any news from the South ? " shouted the one from the Salisbury side. " Yes," was the answer, " Colonel Pennefather is delayed at Fort Tuli." But the roar of the torrent caused this item to be misunderstood and in a few days word reached Salisbury that the Colonel had *died* at Tuli. The flag on the fort was lowered to the half-mast, and, after a decent interval the Colonel's kit, camp furniture and so forth, in accordance with time-honoured custom, was put up to auction, and eagerly snapped up by the junior officers.

The Road to Mashonaland, 1890

A few days later when the floods subsided the Colonel started on his return journey, but before reaching Salisbury encountered one of his subalterns proceeding southward on leave. This young gentleman was so staggered at beholding what at first he thought must be a ghost that he forgot for the moment that he was wearing a pair of excellent field-boots bought at the above-mentioned auction. He partially pulled himself together and attempted a salute. But the Colonel's eyes were sharp. " What the devil do you mean, Sir," he thundered out. " You've got my boots on ! " Nor would he listen to explanations until his trembling junior had taken them off and restored them humbly to their lawful owner.

Those of the Pioneers still living—there are a few—are not likely to forget the hardships which they endured during that wet season in Mashonaland. Many of them on disbandment had formed themselves into prospecting parties, and made camps at Hartley Hill, Mazoe, and in other districts where gold-bearing quartz reefs were reported to exist. They ran up temporary huts built on the native pattern of mud—the only commodity of which there was no lack—and thatch, but such sorry quarters gave little protection against the torrential rains. As no food stuffs could reach them until the roads were open to transport they were on short commons, and had to subsist largely on pumpkins and porridge made of ground native millet—about as appetising as a linseed poultice, which it much resembled. In those days the cause of malaria was unknown, and most of them suffered from repeated attacks of fever. Of course, quinine might have helped them, but the scanty stocks at their command were soon exhausted, and there was no hope of a further supply until communication with the Cape Colony was restored.

At Macloutsie camp in the Northern Protectorate there was a tiny community of nursing Sisters of the Dominican order of the Sacred Heart. To the self-sacrifice and unremitting attention of these ladies, who laboured unceasingly in most trying conditions, many a pioneer owed his life. As soon as transport conditions improved two of them—Mother M. Patrick (whose name became a household word in Rhodesia, and whose memory is still revered) and Sister Amica—travelled by ox-waggon to Fort Salisbury, where they continued their devoted work. It was a rough experience for anyone and must have been exceptionally arduous for two delicately nurtured women, the more so because early in the journey they were left without any guardians except their native servants. Originally they had been placed in the charge of a young Colonial conductor, Van der Riet by name, but they were deprived of his services by a most remarkable accident. He left the waggons one morning to get a shot at a buck, and lost his way in the dense bush. It was a lonely part of the country, and after waiting several days while the natives searched for him, Mother Patrick and her companion were compelled to go on without him. Nothing more was heard of him until six weeks later, when a party of transport riders hunting game in the same neighbourhood caught sight of a wild half-naked creature, who took flight at their approach. They gave chase and captured him, but he was unable to give any account of himself—hardly able indeed to speak ; his teeth were broken, his finger nails worn to the quick, and his clothes reduced to a few rags. It turned out to be Van der Riet, who had been wandering about living on berries and roots for forty days in the wilderness, and had lost his mental faculties. He was soon nursed back to health, but when I saw him shortly after his return to civilisation he had not the smallest recollection of his strange adventure.

Another outstanding figure of that memorable wet season was Dr. Rand, the senior medical officer of the police, who was worked to death attending fever cases in Fort Salisbury and the adjacent camps. For malaria he had a sovereign prescription widely known as " Rand's Kicker." Although one of its ingredients was said to be Cape brandy (at that time a scarce and much-sought restorative), it never became popular as a beverage. Three doses of " Kicker " made one's head buzz like a motor engine, but it did its job.

On his professional rounds Dr. Rand had some queer experiences, one of which is worthy of mention. He had to ride out to Mazoe to attend a fever patient, and when he came to the Gwibi River found it in flood, running bank high. Anxious to keep his clothes and drug-case dry he stripped and made them into a parcel, which he fastened, together with his boots, to the Ds of his saddle. Then with nothing on but his hat he prepared for a swim. He remembered that someone had told him that the best way to cross a river with a horse was to hold on to its tail, and allow the animal to do the hard work and steering. Accordingly, he led it to the water's edge, coaxed it into the river, and took a firm grip of the tail. All went well until they reached the opposite side, when the animal had some difficulty in clambering up the slippery bank, and the doctor unfortunately lost his hold. The horse now refused to be caught, and trotted off in the direction of Mazoe, keeping a little ahead of its master, who hobbled painfully behind. After a few hundred yards one of the boots fell off the saddle, and this he at once put on. A little further on the fellow boot was retrieved in the same manner, but the remaining articles remained in position, and when the two finally arrived at their destination Dr. Rand, although in light marching order, was a bad second.

CHAPTER III.

THE ROAD.

GOODNESS knows why anyone should have wanted to trek up-country after hearing the depressing accounts of Mashonaland which were current in the early months of 1891. For the few rain-sodden mail letters which, after some interruption, reached Cape Colony were gloomy records of flood, famine, and sickness. Of the gold-reefs on which such high hopes had been built we heard next to nothing.

And yet a good many sober-minded people still set their faces northwards, and the applications for posts in the Chartered Company's civil and military establishments still came forward in an incessant stream both from the Colony and from England.

In my own case, though I cannot now see what inducement I had, when the offer was made that I should give up my comfortable job at Kimberley and go to Fort Salisbury as a member of Dr. Jameson's staff I eagerly seized it, and, as soon as the rainy season was over, set out light-heartedly in company with two older men who had also been selected for official billets in the new Territory.

We started from the rail-head at Vryburg in fine style, on a spring-waggon drawn by ten spanking mules, and after many ups and downs two of us crawled into Salisbury, eight weeks later, with the same vehicle—sadly battered, however—behind a span of scraggy cows hired from a transport rider. The third of our party was obliged to return owing to an attack of malarial fever, which in the end proved fatal.

I will not dwell upon the journey of six hundred miles through the monotonous sand and bushveld of Bechuanaland, during which we were often hard pressed to find water for ourselves and our beasts. It was not until we crossed the border and entered the Chartered territory that the real interest began. We halted for a night and a day at Fort Tuli, then the Company's supply base, and, as the last point on the road where parties bound for Mashonaland could repair their waggons and replenish their stores, the scene of much bustle and activity.

The resident population consisted of about a hundred police, and the focus of life was the headquarters mess, presided over by a genial ex-officer of the Inniskilling Dragoons—Captain Tye—who combined in one person the duties of magistrate, commissariat officer, transport officer, postmaster and official host to anybody who had any connection with the Chartered Company and to a great many who had none. We found him extending the hospitality of the mess to an oddly mixed assortment of men—all, more or less, in search of adventure. There were Major Giles, late of the Gunners, and four other members of Lord Randolph Churchill's expedition, the object of which was a mystery to the uninitiated, and even, I am inclined to think, a bit of a puzzle to Lord Randolph himself, who arrived a few days later. There was also Dr. Jameson, fresh back from the Crocodile River, where, by a consummate piece of bluff, he had out-manœuvred a commando of over a hundred Boers who were trying to occupy Mashonaland on their own account— " to jump the Englishman's claim," as they put it. With the " Doctor," as a prisoner on parole, was the Boer Commandant— Colonel Ferreira—a hard-bitten old soldier of fortune, who was now quite as eager to get a job in the Company's service as he had been a week before to lead an expedition to rob it. These and the regular officers of the station made up a cheerful gathering at dinner, and the evening spent at this oasis stands out as one of the most entertaining of my life.

Two of the Churchill party—McKay and Edgell—were excellent banjoists, and several of the company could sing. Major Giles, who was a big handsome man, gave us some of the latest comic songs from England, including " The Bogey Man." He had dined well, and had worked himself up into a rather excited condition. Whilst singing the chorus—" Hush ! Hush !! Hush ! ! ! Here comes the Bogey Man ! "—he stalked round the half-lit mess hut with what he imagined to be appropriate pantomime, but upon his face coming unexpectedly into contact with the clammy surface of a canvas water-cooler hanging in the shadow his overwrought feelings gave way ; he uttered a yell of terror and subsided on the floor.

At Tuli I also met an old Balliol friend—Victor Morier— who gave us the story of the spirited little battle between a troop of the Chartered Pioneers under Captain Heyman and the Portuguese garrison at Massi Kessi, close to the frontier of Manicaland. Morier had been present at this, and having a good knowledge of Portuguese (acquired at Lisbon, where his father had spent some years as British Minister), had acted as interpreter. He told us that when Heyman's half-starved soldiers occupied Massi Kessi fort after its evacuation they found it replete with all sorts of stores and luxuries, including a great number of demi-johns of *vinho tinto* and a quantity of ladies' silk under-garments. Morier was on his way to England, but died on the homeward voyage, to the great grief of all who knew him.

After our parched and dusty trek through Bechuanaland it was a pleasant change to get into the broken and well-watered country between Tuli and the next station—Fort Victoria, two hundred miles to the north-east. There were plenty of natives along this part of the road, but they were a miserable lot, and still lived in the state of thraldom to which they had been brought by fifty years of Matabele raids and persecution. Their villages were invariably perched in the most inaccessible granite kopjes, and could only be reached by rough ladders and steep and tortuous paths known only to themselves. There was always a look-out man on the highest crag to signal the approach of strangers, and, when he gave the alarm, the whole population of the village would scramble up into safety, driving before them their herds of pygmy goats and cattle. If they were reassured, a few of the bolder men would cautiously descend with meal, sweet potatoes and absurd little cocks and hens for sale, and would be followed gradually by the women and children. With money they were not then familiar. The only coin they knew was a shilling, and this was quoted as the price of all commodities, regardless of quality or size. A goat was " a shilling," and so was a fowl, and even an egg. But they much preferred bartering for trade goods, such as red beads with white eyes, coarse blue calico known as " limbo," cheap cotton shirts and blankets, and brass cartridge cases, which they used as snuff-boxes. They were of mild disposition and easily scared, taking flight like wild animals at any suspicious movement on our part.

Every fifty miles or so we came upon a lonely post of two or three police troopers, whose regular duties were not so engrossing as to prevent them from fraternising with us at the outspan, listening to the news and sharing our camp meals, sometimes even accompanying us for a few miles of the road. The boredom of their lives must have been appalling. They could shoot game, of course, but seldom found the energy to do so, though it would have meant a respite from the eternal " bully beef," which formed the staple of their rations. They generally tried to impress us with thrilling stories of lions and other beasts of prey

Our Waggon, 1891

to be encountered on the road. Several times we did, in fact, hear the roar of lions or found their spoor on the dusty track, and, as we were told of their partiality for mule, we generally built bush *scherms* round our camp at night and kept good fires burning, but we never got a sight of one.

In one of the parties we overtook on the way was a youth fresh from England, who had been equipped by some London outfitter with all that fancy could devise in the sporting line. Round his waist was a leather hunting-belt, complete with bowie knife, field-glasses and revolver. There was buckskin strapping at his knees and on the shoulders of his Norfolk jacket. He wore a dandy pair of field-boots, and carried an eye-glass. He never stirred without his rifle, and his one absorbing idea was to bag a lion. All this was an irresistible temptation to his companions, who warned him that the country near the Lundi River was noted for lions, which were to be seen prowling about in every direction. Accordingly, when the party drew near the danger zone, our young friend, who was not devoid of pluck, hurried on ahead of the waggon, and spent some hours tramping through the bush with his rifle at the " ready," but without a glimpse of what he was looking for. Eventually he came upon a police post, and, entering one of the huts, found a corporal and two troopers sitting down at their tea. " Er—where are the lions ? " he enquired, fixing his monocle in his eye. The corporal was equal to the occasion. Springing smartly to attention, he saluted and replied : " They'll be in at six o'clock, sir. We don't stable them at night ; we just knee-halter them and let them run."

To reach Mashonaland all travellers had, in 1891, to follow the new road cut a few months previously by the pioneer column under the guidance of the famous hunter, F. C. Selous. In order to avoid the possibility of giving offence to the Matabele—in those days regarded with a respect almost amounting to dread—the column had kept to the low-lying bush-veld on the eastern side of their boundaries. It was a hot, unhealthy district, watered by many fair-sized rivers, on whose banks were a few palms and other tropical trees, while hippopotamuses and crocodiles were said to infest the pools, though we never saw them. The most prominent features of the landscape were the dome-like hills of solid granite, nude of all vegetation, standing out boldly from the rocky ridges which intersected the country in every direction. One of these was Savana Buli, a grey peak like a gigantic sugar-loaf, towering seven hundred feet above the surrounding plain. Halfway up its slope was a dark patch marking a cave, which, the natives asserted, was the entrance to a tunnel running right through the solid mass. But white men regarded this as a myth.

After the conquest of the Matabele in 1893, the Selous road was replaced by an easier and more direct route across the high veld from Salisbury to Bulawayo ; and as no one but a few traders settled in the low country, the highway carved with such pains by the pioneers was abandoned and forgotten. Twenty-four years later, in the course of some wanderings in the native districts, I came upon it once more. The track was overgrown by bush, but the ruts made by the waggons of the early trekkers, and deepened into watercourses by the heavy rains, were still visible in parts. One afternoon four of us were camped at the foot of the "Sugar-loaf Kopje," and the old native legend was recalled. Two of our party decided to put the existence of a tunnel to the test, and some bets were made. We watched them with our glasses scramble up to the dark patch and vanish into a recess, and, sure enough, an hour later they reappeared on the opposite face of the hill. They had proved the truth of the rumour and won their bet, but at the cost of a bad scare, for near the mouth of the tunnel they had come upon a full-grown leopard—a nasty customer to disturb in the semi-darkness.

To return to our journey ; in 1891 the road made by the column was the only means of reaching Fort Salisbury. A fortnight after leaving Tuli we reached the precipitous defile— known as "Providence Gorge"—by which Selous had guided the Pioneers to the high veld. Two days were occupied in coaxing our worn-out mules up this difficult mountain pass, and then at last we emerged on the high plateau of Mashonaland.

Nothing could be more sudden or striking than the transition from the humid, thickly-wooded low veld, which we had left 1,500 feet below, to the spacious champaign which now stretched ahead of us as far as the eye could reach. In spite of the powerful sunshine, the crisp air was like a tonic, and we felt fresh and invigorated. There was not a sign of life beyond two rows of wattle and daub huts for the police detachment and a tiny fort which the Pioneers had thrown up to guard the mouth of the pass, and over which the Union Jack was bravely fluttering. This was Fort Victoria, destined, two years later, to be the scene of the first brush between the Mashonaland settlers and the young braves of Lobengula's army.

From now onwards we had more company on the road. Almost daily we overtook parties of prospectors who had started long before from Kimberley, and had been delayed, sometimes for weeks, by swollen rivers. At our nightly halts we usually found the camps of other travellers, all bound for the same goal, eager to hear the latest news from the South and to exchange gossip about the experiences of the journey.

The freemasonry of the road gave us introduction to some picturesque characters. There was "Harry the Reefer," for instance, a rolling stone, who had come out to the Diamond fields in 1871 and had been a prospector at Malmani, Barberton, and every other mining camp in South Africa. A chronic affection of the right elbow had prevented him from making money, but he had amassed a store of surprising information on geology, natural history and veld lore which he was ready to impart to any one who would stand him a drink. The first time we fell in with him we were outspanned on the edge of a vley where the mosquitoes were more than usually vicious. It may, of course, have been a pure accident that his appearance coincided with the moment when we were just preparing for our daily " sundowner." At any rate he sat down on his roll of blankets and unstrapped a grimy and battered tin pannikin. We satisfied his immediate needs and watched him extract some rank tobacco from a little bag dangling at his waist-belt and fill and light an ancient pipe. After the first few puffs we noticed that all the mosquitoes had beat a hasty retreat from our neighbourhood.

" Musketeers," said Harry. " You don't call them there gnats ' musketeers ' do you ? You should a seen 'em down on the Komati River when I was there in '86. They was so so big that one of 'em could kill a sea-cow (hippopotamus). But he couldn't get him to the bank. No. It took two of 'em to tow him ashore."

This was an encouraging start, and we got on to the subject of insect pests in general, with which, both wild and domesticated, he claimed to have a close acquaintance. " Now there's tetse fly," he observed. " Their poison is very virtulent. But I carries about a bottle of Croft's snake-bite tincture. That's the best anecdote I knows of against the virtulent poison of the tetse fly."

Harry had done a bit of big game hunting in his time, and his stories gained a certain piquancy from his use of unexpected expressions.

" Shyest kind of buck," he told us, " is them there bastard hartybeast (tsessebe.) You can't never get within range of 'em. Onst I spent half a day stalking an old bull out Lomagundi way. Over kopjes and across vleys, one moment in thorn bush and next in grass over your head. At last I got a sight of him standing out in the open, about half a mile off as I reckoned. I put up the 900 yards and drew a bead on him and when I let off I seen him drop in his tracks. Took me best part of twenty minutes to get up to him. But he warn't dead. Oh no, only paralysed. I must have aimed a bit high 'cos I found my bullet had just grazed the vibrerta of his neck."

Another road acquaintance—but of a very different type—was " Captain " Bullock, who caught us up with half a dozen horses which he was taking to Fort Salisbury to sell. Of debonair appearance and irreproachable manners, he was generally supposed—and he did not contradict the rumour—to be closely connected with the Peerage ; and indeed we were allowed to see that he carried in his wallets a pair of ivory hair-brushes marked with coronets. From other sources, however, we were led to believe that he was an accomplished horse thief, and one or two of his escapades gave colour to this idea. At a later date he made a journey to the Zambesi and returned to Salisbury with circumstantial evidence of valuable coal deposits which he had located in his travels, in proof of which he exhibited about a hundred-weight of coal which he had in a box on his waggon, and which, on being tested, gave excellent results. A well-known financial magnate who was on the look-out for promising properties was so much interested that he advanced him two hundred pounds to make a second expedition to secure the ground. This was the last he saw of Bullock, and it transpired afterwards that he had obtained his samples from the bunkers of a small steamer plying on the river, with the connivance of her German engineer who was a party to the plot, Bullock eventually went out of his mind and became the victim of embarrassing delusions. From a long habit of pretending to be a person of social importance, he arrived at last at the conviction that he was of Divine origin.

Long before we reached Salisbury the mules which had made so brave a start from Vryburg gave in. Two or three died of poverty and the rest were so weak that we had to leave them at Charter—a spot situated in a sandy waste where for some obscure reason the authorities had built a third and utterly useless fort garrisoned at the time of our arrival by a detachment of listless police. Fortunately we made friends with some transport riders who had a few cows trained to the yoke, and with eight of these we accomplished the last stages of the journey. One of our original animals, less poverty-stricken than the rest, we brought on with us tied to the tail of the waggon, but a party of lions visited our camp one night at the Umfuli River, and in the general confusion and uproar the mule broke away and was never seen by us again, though we heard afterwards that Captain Bullock got him all right.

Speaking of lions reminds me that before starting we were told that whatever else might be scarce along the road we should find no lack of fresh meat, for the whole country was teeming with herds of big game. On this advice we laid in a large stock of ammunition and left " bully-beef " out of our commissariat. Had it not been that birds were plentiful we should have fared badly, for in the whole course of the journey we actually saw but one head—a sable antelope bull, which came and stared at us at a moment when we were both bathing and, of course, had no rifles.

At last, after sixty days of travelling, we reached the " seat of Government," and were glad enough to make our final outspan in a clump of trees close to the spot where the Salisbury Club now stands. A description of the camp as we found it must be left to the next chapter.

CHAPTER IV.

A City in Embryo.

JUST before leaving Cape Colony we had seen a copy of
"SOUTH AFRICA," with a map in which the name FORT
SALISBURY was printed in the thick type usually associated
with flourishing capital cities. Nevertheless it would have
been easy, at the time of our arrival, to pass within a few
hundred yards of the place itself without noticing it. The
surrounding country was clothed with a dense growth of coarse
grass five feet or more in height. From this emerged a low
tree-covered hill—the " Kopje "—at the foot of which were
a couple of score of thatched huts hardly differing from those
of the native kraals we had seen on the road. This was the
" business " quarter of the township. A mile or so away were
other groups of huts, in some of which Dr. Jameson and his
new staff lived, messed and carried on the work of " Government." The Police quarters looked like cow-sheds, and were
arranged round an earth-work—the Fort—above which flew
the Union Jack charged with the Company's badge of a golden
lion. Scattered here and there were canvas tents, waggons
protected by buck-sails, and the frameworks of more huts in
process of erection.

The two main camps were separated by a dismal black
swamp, the haunt of snipe and the noisy rendezvous of innumerable frogs. It was afterwards drained, and is now traversed
by a fine broadway in which stand the Town-hall and other
substantial buildings, but in those early days it was almost
impassable in the rainy season, even on horseback.

Four or five hundred sun-burnt young men, clad for the
most part in flannel shirts, weather-beaten corduroy breeches
and broad-brimmed slouch hats—the type beloved by lady
novelists—constituted the population of Fort Salisbury. There
was said to be a white woman somewhere in the camp, but she
must have remained in *purdah*, for we never saw her. The
only local " institutions " were the English Church and the
weekly newspaper ; but of these more hereafter.

Part of the inducement held out to me before starting had
been the promise of " Government Quarters, rent free," and I

Government Offices, Salisbury, 1891

(Dr. Jameson's office on right.)

made all speed to find Dr. Harris, the Secretary of the Company, to ascertain their whereabouts. With the air of one who had devoted many hours of thought to this problem, he pointed to a vacant space on the veld—there was really no lack of vacant spaces—and said, " That's where I advise you to build your hut." He was also good enough to indicate a clump of trees where I could cut the requisite poles, and a pit where the right kind of mud could be procured. In the course of our conversation he made it clear that if I wanted a bed, a table or any other article of furniture I should have to make it myself out of logs hewn from the neighbouring woods, for no manufactured goods were obtainable in camp, and, except food, of which the need was greatest, nothing would be brought up from the South for months to come. (This, by the way, proved a false prophecy, for the earliest waggons to arrive invariably carried cargoes of whiskey.)

The prospect of spending the first few weeks of my new appointment in cutting grass, chopping poles and daubing them with dagga* was not inspiring, but mercifully, on that very day, Mr. Colquhoun, the Administrator, who had resigned his post, started down country, and I at once appropriated his roomy hut, which contained a bed supported on poles driven into the ground and other similar " fixtures." To make my tenure more secure I took in as lodger, and promptly put to bed, a new acquaintance, Jim Kennedy, who was down with fever and too ill to be moved. By this means I was enabled to hold my quarters against other claimants, and by the time the sick man was convalescent my title was fairly established.

The total absence at first of all imported goods led to strange results. We, the Company's servants, were all drawing rations, and as there was nothing to buy we were unable to spend our pay in the ordinary way, and frittered it away in poker, nap or faro, and in the most insane speculation.

A few enterprising spirits formed an Hotel Company, the shares in which were eagerly competed for, and were bought and sold, before the hotel itself became a reality, at prices far beyond their nominal value. As a special favour one of the Directors allowed me to take over two of his own shares at £15 each, and warmly congratulated me upon my good fortune at having " got in on the ground floor." When the hotel was eventually built it was all " ground floor "—merely a long barn-like structure of pole and dagga containing extensive bar

* Dagga—a Kaffir word for a kind of mortar composed of mud mixed with cow-dung.

accommodation but little else. It did no business at all until a few waggon loads of whiskey arrived, when it leapt into a sudden prosperity, which seemed to augur fat dividends for the lucky shareholders. But, alas! the camaraderie which grew up between its manager and its thirsty patrons wrecked our prospects. Customers were allowed to obtain drinks by the simple process of signing cards, or, as we called them, " Good-fors." When the flood of whiskey abated and the affairs of the Mashonaland Hotel Company were investigated, it was found that the liquid assets had been entirely converted into paper, the cards of one droughty pioneer alone amounting to a total of £187. To crown all we shareholders learnt that the Company had never been registered, which meant that our liability was unlimited. My " ground floor " position cost me another £20 per share, and the fact that the Hotel Company held seven shillings worth of my own cards seemed a very inadequate consolation.

Mention of " good-fors " recalls the surprising conditions created by the dearth of coin, which in the first year or two after the occupation was more scarce than any other commodity. Its place was taken by cheques, and as the nearest bank was at Mafeking and the post took four weeks to reach it and four weeks to return, there was a distinct risk in accepting the paper of anybody not in a settled position. The Chartered Company's cheques were the recognised and standard currency, but, as they were often for odd amounts, business transactions, even with their assistance, were complicated and exasperating.

One day news reached our mess that the surplus stores of a mining syndicate, consisting—it was said—mainly of "luxuries," were to be sold by auction, and I was deputed to attend the sale, obtaining a morning's release from duty for this purpose. The available funds of the mess consisted of a Company's cheque for £5 3s. 4d., which was handed to me with earnest injunctions to invest it with discretion. I found about a hundred miners, transport riders and police troopers gathered round Charlie Maddocks, the pioneer auctioneer, who was disposing of a mixed collection of old clothes, bags of Kaffir meal, mining tools and other junk. After several disappointments I made a successful bid of 17s. 6d. for about 50 lbs. of potatoes. These were indeed a luxury, and I joyfully tendered the cheque for £5 3s. 4d. " No change," said Maddocks, " but we'll soon put that right," and before I grasped the situation he had put up, and knocked down to me—though I had not uttered a word—a pair of second-hand field boots for £2 10s. and a bottle of Cape brandy for £1. He then offered to toss me double or quits for the balance of 15s

—no one bothered about pence in those times—and on my winning offered me the choice between another bottle of " dop " and somebody else's doubtful cheque for 25s. I innocently took the latter, but it was not without much trouble that I eventually induced a third party to accept it in exchange for a pound of Boer tobacco. The other members of the mess expressed themselves somewhat forcibly when they learnt the result of my morning's shopping. Very grudgingly they passed the expenditure on potatoes, dop and tobacco, but they utterly repudiated the boots, which I was compelled to take over. They didn't fit me, and were eventually accepted by my native servant in lieu of a month's wages.

These Saturday auctions on the market square became regular institutions in Rhodesia. Every conceivable kind of movable property, from a bullock wagon to a saucepan with a hole in it, was brought to them. Articles of domestic furniture frequently appeared which had become familiar from having passed through the hands of many successive owners, and, as with old masters or noted *objets d'art*, the prices they had fetched at previous sales were remembered and quoted. Horses— occasionally sound, but more often in an advanced state of decrepitude—were also common features of the sales, and provided excellent opportunities for an exchange of chaff between the crowd of buyers and idlers and the auctioneers, of whom Charlie Maddocks was perhaps the most nimble-witted. Only once do I remember his being at a loss for a repartee. He was putting up an ancient screw and by prodigious efforts had raised the bidding to £7. Several times he had shouted, " Going at seven ! For the last time at seven ! " when old Mackinley, a well-known horse-dealer, strolled across the square and stopped to have a look. Charlie paused, and kept his hammer in mid-air while Mackinley gravely walked round the horse. Somewhat encouraged, Charlie resumed his appeal. " Going at seven ! " he shouted, once more. Mackinley removed his pipe and spat. " I'll make it seven-and-six," he said.

And now for the local " institutions." At first there was only one " Church "—that started by the English chaplain, Canon Balfour, afterwards Bishop of Bloemfontein. The Jesuit Fathers followed shortly afterwards, and within a few months the Wesleyans and other denominations appeared on the scene.

Poor Canon Balfour had an uphill task. Besides being single handed, he was torn between the duty imposed upon him by his Mission of Christianising the natives and that of ministering to the spiritual needs of the pioneers with whom he had arrived and among whom he had made his friends. I think that his inclinations were towards the latter, but he bravely made several expeditions on foot into the native districts. As a missionary to the heathen he was set a hopeless task. What possible impression could one man make upon hundreds of thousands of savages scattered over an area the size of France and steeped in witchcraft and the grossest forms of paganism? He had no money, no means of travelling—not even a horse. His Bishop, Dr. Knight-Bruce, had made one or two visits to the country, but was now in England, lecturing and preaching with the object of raising funds for the prosecution of the missionary side of the work of the Anglican Church. At no time, then or afterwards, did the Bishop make any attempt at permanent residence in his diocese, and though he was a man of commanding presence and a powerful speaker, he never became a familiar figure in the life of the early pioneers. His efforts to form a community of nursing sisters at Umtali were amusingly described in a book written by two English girls who were induced to undertake the unknown and perilous eastern route to Mashonaland on the assurance of the Bishop that everything had been made ready for them.

Canon Balfour was rather a pathetic figure during his two years' sojourn in Salisbury. A devout, but retiring and somewhat austere, man, he never seemed quite at home among the mixed crowd of miners, traders and speculators who formed the bulk of the community. The services which he held in the little mud church—built by himself with the assistance of two or three friends—were always well attended, however, and the congregation saw nothing incongruous in the homely fittings, also made by the Canon with his own hands out of such scanty materials as he could find about him. The altar was a large packing case covered with blue trade calico ; the lectern a smaller case, on one side of which the stencilled words " Milkmaid Brand " were still visible and betrayed its original purpose. Outside the building was a steel drill suspended from a frame of poles. This was the church bell, which the Canon used patiently to toll on Sundays by striking it with a cold chisel for a quarter of an hour before each service.

The Jesuits also had at first a single representative— Father Hartmann, a jovial monk, as broad as he was long, and a great favourite with all. He was mainly engaged in preparing a dictionary and grammar of the Mashona language and in selecting stations for the important mission which the Roman Catholic Church soon after established, with branches extending over the whole colony, and with allied communities of nuns engaged in nursing and educational work.

Strangely enough, the third mission to arrive was one sent by the Salvation Army, consisting of a " Major," who was accompanied by his wife and two little daughters—the first white children to make their appearance. As religious workers they made little headway, for the white population was not of the class to which the revivalist meetings of the Army were likely to appeal, and the problem of converting the natives was too big for two or three individuals, however enthusiastic, to tackle. They held a few services at the outset and actually gained a few recruits. One of these was a stalwart young pioneer who was not particularly noted for asceticism or extreme piety in his mode of living. It was rumoured that Donaldson (that was not his name) intended publicly to make a profession of his repentance at the next meeting, and a number of his friends rallied to the Salvation Army headquarters, curious to see whether he would face the music. Sure enough, the new convert rose and announced that he had been " saved " and intended thenceforth to lead a new life. " This," he said smiting his chest with great impressiveness, " is not the old Donaldson who is addressing you, but an entirely new Donaldson ! " whereat one of the unregenerates at the back of the room interrupted, with an inquiry—" Will the new Donaldson pay the old Donaldson's debts ? "

The Salvation Army contingent afterwards devoted some of their energies to more mundane pursuits. At a later date the Major gained great distinction for gallant conduct in the native rebellion and also became one of the early Mayors of Salisbury.

The earliest newspaper in Rhodesia was the *Mashonaland Herald and Zambesian Times*. It was a weekly news sheet written, printed, published and distributed by one man, Mr. W. E. Fairbridge, whose indomitable pluck in face of endless discouragements deserves an honourable place in the history of journalistic enterprise. He employed some sort of cyclostyle process which reproduced his actual handwriting, but his mechanical appliances, which included a tray of sticky jelly and an ink roller, were not of the same high quality as his intellectual outfit. The ink, which he made himself, was generally to blame. Sometimes there was a superabundance of black pigment and the *Herald* looked as if it had passed through the office of a Russian press-censor. On other occasions an excess of oil gave it the appearance of having been wrapped round a pat of butter. For the early editions Fairbridge was obliged to use any paper that he could buy, beg or borrow locally, and he achieved a great triumph when he managed to obtain a part-used ledger and brought out an edition ruled with double money columns in red.   It was a refreshing sight to see him on the morning of publication delivering the papers on horseback to his patrons, whose subscriptions—such as were paid at all— took the form of a packet of candles or a pot of marmalade—in one instance, he told me, an old spade.

Through all these vicissitudes the *Herald* held its own.   It soon became a printed paper and under a slightly different name has continued to make a regular appearance until the present time, when it is one of the leading journals in the whole of Africa.

Once a week—though at no certain hour or even day—a two-wheeled cart, drawn by six oxen and driven by a police trooper in brown corduroy uniform, used to lumber into Fort Salisbury.   As soon as it was noticed crawling round the end of the kopje there was a general rush to the Government side of the camp, for this was the English mail, and, for most of us, meant letters from our people at home and news of the outer world.

The pioneer postmaster was an imperturbable Colonial who never allowed himself to be hustled out of his official calm by the impatience of the general public.   He cultivated this virtue to such an extent that eventually it gained him the recognition of his superiors.   It happened in this wise.   The mail cart arrived one evening at a moment when he was sitting down to an appetising dinner of roast buck.   He bade the driver take off the bags and deposit them inside the hut, then locked the door and resumed his interrupted meal.   Meanwhile the crowd outside grew larger and more importunate and when some of them peeped through the window and saw the postmaster at dinner their exasperation knew no bounds.   But he steadily munched on with sublime indifference until shouts of " Break the door open ! " " Tear the roof off ! " led him to consider that the time for departmental activity had arrived.   Then rapidly cutting the strings of two of the mail bags, he shook the contents out of the window.   " There you are ! " he cried, " sort them yourselves, you lousy blighters ! "

The Mashonaland Herald & Zambesian Times

No. 31 Salisbury, Saturday 23 Jan 1892

Morris, Campbell and Cornwall
Auctioneers, Accountants, Agents
& Wholesale Merchants

beg to announce that they are now prepared to supply provisions of all descriptions at exceptionally low rates, to dealers only.

Price lists for current month on application.

The Auctioneering Business of Mr M. H. Morris will be carried on as usual under the name of the above firm, as also the accountancy & secretarial business of Messrs Campbell & Cornwall.

The Earliest Newspaper

CHAPTER V.

" The Doctor."

THE life and soul of all the activity of preparation which
kept Mashonaland busy in its first year was the man whom
everyone—whites and natives alike—knew as " the Doctor."

Let me try and give a picture of Jameson as he was then—
four years before the tragedy which made him, for a space,
the most talked of man in the world ; which made him appear
to some the Paladin of a righteous cause, to others a mischievous
marauder of the most dangerous type.

Since 1889, when he forsook a lucrative medical practice
in Kimberley and made his first journey from Cape Colony to
Matabeleland to prepare the mind of the Chief Lobengula for
the occupation of part of his country, he had been incessantly
on the move. People who travel in the modern saloon coaches
of the Rhodesia Railway and reach Bulawayo sixty or seventy
hours after leaving the coast, with no greater discomfort than
a certain amount of heat and dust in passing through Bechuanaland, can have no idea of the trying conditions of the same
journey in the days when, north of Kimberley, the ox-waggon
and the mule-cart were the only means of conveyance. Jameson
had made this seven-hundred-mile trek over the veld three
times in Rhodes' interests. He had also accompanied the
Pioneers on their famous march, and, at its conclusion, had
explored the route from Mashonaland to the east coast, through
country infested with tsetse fly and reeking of malaria, until
he reached what is now the port of Beira. In the following
year he had made a still more hazardous and exhausting journey
across country to Gazaland, and had suffered the indignity of
capture by the Portuguese for trespassing on their long-
cherished, but quite legendary, claims to that country. Finally,
he had rushed down to the Crocodile River to turn back a
threatened Boer raid on Mashonaland. (Was there not, in the
light of later events, a certain grim irony in this last achievement ?)

Few men could have come unscathed through such ordeals,
and in Jameson, who started with a splendid constitution, the
hardships and exposure he had undergone sowed the seeds of

29

maladies from which he never really recovered, and which undoubtedly shortened his life. In 1891 he was no longer robust. At times he suffered acute pain. He had also acquired a slightly anxious or weary expression, which was never wholly absent from his face even when lit up, as it generally was, by his irresistible smile.

When, at Rhodes' request, and by way of a " rest," he undertook the government of the young colony and settled down to official duties at Salisbury, he was in his thirty-ninth year. Rather below the average height, he carried himself with a slight stoop. His attitudes were always careless. When mounted on his brown cob " Moscow " he rode with slack rein and loose leg. Dismounted he was inclined to lounge, with his hands in his pockets. His outward mien betrayed no sign of the feverish restlessness which coursed through his veins. Yet the mainspring of the Doctor's life was a fierce activity—not impulsiveness so much as a deliberate craving for movement, risk and adventure.

Utterly unversed in official routine, he now bent himself to the task of organising departments of Government—not, however, government on the approved lines followed in older colonies, which would have been unsuitable for a community consisting of a handful of young Englishmen suddenly let loose amid a population of aboriginal savages, but government based on a rough and ready intuition, heedless of precedents, elastic, creating rules from day to day to meet the needs of the moment. He took a hand in every branch of administration. Were there legal cases to be tried, Jameson was ready to try them, and to dispense with law books, juries and prosecutors, confident in his own common-sense to carry him through. Were problems of economy to be faced, Jameson, whose experience of finance was never equal to the strain of keeping his private accounts in order, promptly tackled them, and proved as adroit at cutting down expenditure as he was at amputating legs.

The Imperial Government had sanctioned the appointment of half-a-dozen of the police officers as district Resident Magistrates, and Jameson himself was gazetted Chief Magistrate, with powers equal to a High Court Judge. There were seldom any cases serious enough to justify High Court proceedings, but once or twice he heard petty cases in the local court at Salisbury when the regular Magistrate, Major Forbes, was absent on some other duty. On these occasions I, as his private secretary, filled the rôle of Clerk of the Court, and, on the strength of a very slight acquaintance with English procedure,

Hon. C. White.   Col. F. Rhodes.   " The Doctor."   Hon. H. F. White.
A Salisbury Group, 1894

endeavoured to keep the Doctor within bounds. But it was no easy matter, for he had a contempt for formality, and preferred to cut through legal tangles by novel methods of his own. There was the case, for instance, of an Indian coolie who accused another coolie of fraud. A long string of hard-swearing witnesses had been suborned on either side, and it eventually became apparent that the charge was a trumped-up one, brought from vindictive motives. Jameson thereupon brought the proceedings to an abrupt conclusion by sentencing the *prosecutor* to receive ten lashes and several of his principal witnesses five lashes each. For a long time after that startling but admirably just decision vexatious indictments were unknown in the Salisbury Court.

Jameson could, however, rise to the occasion if necessary, and I have never forgotten the dignified way in which he conducted the trial of the first murder case heard in Rhodesia, and the only one to this day which has resulted in the hanging of a European. The accused was a Jew from Holland, and the evidence against him was circumstantial, but conclusive. In sentencing the wretched man to death Jameson, who was assisted by four assessors, spoke with great impressiveness and evident emotion, and in forwarding the records of the trial for confirmation by the High Commissioner at Cape Town he gave a lucid and thoughtful summary of the evidence and of his reasons for the decision.

In his intercourse with those around him Jameson was no stickler for etiquette. His chief weapon was good-humoured banter, but this was only a cloak for a real and personal sympathy which won him the confidence and affection of the circle of varied characters which the Pioneer expedition had brought together, and kept the discordant elements not only in good order but in good temper. His everyday work of administration was transacted in a large square thatched hut, with walls of poles and mud, lined and ceiled with native-made mats of split bamboo. Here, with his feet on the table in front of him, with his chair tilted back, and with a cigarette between his fingers, he would receive deputations and chat with callers, official or otherwise. They generally came to air some grievance, but were disarmed by the shrewd and friendly chaff which they encountered, and, though seldom gaining their point, they invariably left in sublime good temper.

In October, 1891, Rhodes came up by the East Coast route to pay his first visit to the colony which he had founded, and particularly to confer with the Doctor on the subject of finance.

For the Company's funds were running low, and hardly any revenue was to be expected for months to come. The most ruinous item of expenditure was the cost, amounting to about £150,000 a year, of the police force which the Imperial authorities required the Company to maintain as a safeguard against attacks from the natives, and Rhodes and Jameson put their heads together to devise some means of ridding themselves of this white elephant. They pooh-poohed the notion that the settlers, who were mostly men in the prime of their vigour, accustomed to firearms, and thoroughly used to taking care of themselves, required a permanent body of six hundred police to protect them from the invertebrate native tribes of Mashonaland, who were so craven that a white man armed with nothing more lethal than a sjambok could put to flight a score of them. This, in fact, was what we all felt. We had yet to learn the capacity for mischief that was latent in natives even of the blandest exterior.

There were, of course, the Matabele, just over the border, but a year had passed since the Occupation, and they had shown no overt sign of hostility. To the majority of the settlers the Matabele menace was a burst bubble. The few who wagged their heads and said : " Don't be too cocksure ! " were laughed at as scaremongers. The man who could speak with authority was Jameson himself, who had lived among the Matabele and knew their character. He assured everyone that King Lobengula was desperately anxious to avoid war, and that, as long as white men did not encroach upon Matabeleland proper, Lobengula would be strong enough to hold his young bloods in check. And so the little community was lulled into a fool's paradise, and went about its business of farming and prospecting in twos and threes all over the country with easy indifference to the thunder-clouds on the horizon, and the Doctor proceeded with his " economies."

The commissioned ranks of the police were filled by officers seconded from the Regular Army or Militia, whose chief aim was, naturally, to keep their men in a high state of military efficiency by constant drills and training. This Jameson regarded as mere show. He could not understand why the Company, which was paying for the force, should not call upon its members to perform civil duties, such as driving post-carts, carrying chains for surveyors, or doing clerical work in the administrative offices. As I once heard him put it to the Commanding Officer : " When your men are doing nothing, you show them in your returns as ' available for duty ' ! But the moment I ask for a man to do something, I am told that he must get extra duty pay."

Both he and Rhodes realised, however, that the Colonial Office had to be considered, and would be unlikely to consent to the disbandment, or even reduction, of the police unless assured that there was something to take its place. Under the " Burgher Law " of Cape Colony, which was in force in Mashonaland, all able-bodied citizens were liable to be called on to take up arms at times of public danger ; but this could hardly be regarded as justification for abolishing the police by a stroke of the pen, which was what Jameson would have liked to do.

In the long run it was arranged to raise a force of Volunteers at Salisbury and Victoria and to reduce the police from six hundred and fifty to one hundred and fifty of all ranks. And Jameson promised Rhodes to effect the change by the end of 1891.

There was a good deal of amusement about the formation of the " Mashonaland Horse "—for nothing less than a mounted force would have attracted volunteers. A number of meetings were held in a new brick hotel which had just been built in Salisbury, and a good deal of whiskey was consumed at Jameson's expense. Whiskey was so expensive and difficult to obtain that the temptation of free drinks was an unfailing lure. By this means, and by the promise of horses, Jameson succeeded before Christmas in enrolling several hundred men in his harum-scarum regiment, including a number of the disbanded policemen. The authorities at the Colonial Office were consulted only when the arrangements had been completed. They were rather taken aback, but were loth to object too strongly for fear of furnishing the Company with a pretext for claiming Imperial protection at the expense of the British Exchequer. It was another case of successful bluff on the part of the Doctor.

The Mashonaland Horse was at first little more than a paper regiment. Everyone wanted to be an officer, or at least a sergeant, and those who did not obtain distinction of this sort were not very zealous in attending the musters. At one of the first parades there were present the commanding officer (Major Forbes), the adjutant (Major " Maori " Browne), a sprinkling of captains and lieutenants, quite a considerable body of quartermaster-sergeants, provost-sergeants, paymaster sergeants, bombardiers (we had an artillery section), farriers, and so on—and one trooper, who happened to be the present writer. Eventually some remounts were brought up from the south and the movement became more popular. The horses were handed over to those volunteers who would undertake to feed and look after them, but most of them were in very low condition after the long journey from Cape Colony, and our Farrier-Major, Wignall, had his work cut out to get them fit for duty. He possessed no instruments and very few medicines, but he was not lacking in resource. Once a week the volunteers were required to bring their horses to him for inspection, and one morning he decided that a particular animal required a physic ball. He had no balling-pistol, but produced a length of india-rubber tubing and a ball, and instructed the man how to perform the operation. " You grasp the horse's tongue," he explained, " and pull it out on the off side of its lower jaw. Then put the ball in the tube and insert one end as far back as possible in the pharynx. Put the other end in your own mouth and blow hard. Do you understand ? " The trooper said he thought he did, and went off. A day or two later he turned up again with his horse, which did not seem to have derived much benefit from the treatment, while this time the man himself looked exceedingly unwell. " Did you carry out my instructions ? " said Wignall. " Well, I did my best," was the reply. " I got the tube down the horse's throat all right, but the silly beggar blew first ! "

As soon as the remounts were fit, Major Forbes gave orders for a general inspection parade on the racecourse, at which Jameson consented to take the salute. The majority of the volunteers were thoroughly at home in the saddle, but there were two or three novices whose performances were a sore trial to the patience of the Commanding Officer and Adjutant. We went through the usual advance in review order—first at the walk and finally at the canter, which proved rather an undignified stampede. When the dust cleared away, one unlucky trooper was discovered sitting on the ground, well in rear of the line, ruefully watching his mount which was careering back to the stables. The adjutant galloped up and addressed him. " What the —— do you propose to do now, you —— little image ? " he shouted. The dismounted one picked himself up and saluted. " I propose to resign, sir," he meekly answered.

However, the Mashonaland Horse was still a live body when the trouble arose at Victoria which eventually led to the Matabele War, and as soon as there was a prospect of active service all ranks strove ardently to make themselves efficient. Military experts were of opinion that a force of five thousand trained soldiers was the smallest that could safely be employed against Lobengula's veterans, but Jameson's gambling instinct impelled him to make the attempt to occupy Matabeleland with his seven hundred men, which was all he could raise in Salisbury and Victoria, assisted by two or three hundred more volunteers

brought up from the south and—rather against his inclination
—by a contingent of about two hundred of the trained police
from Bechuanaland. The Mashonaland Horse were put through
about a month's training under service conditions and took the
field, with very inadequate provision in the shape of transport
and ordnance, in October, 1893. The factor upon which
Jameson banked was surprise, and this, combined with a strong
element of good luck, enabled him to bring what most people
thought a desperate venture to a brilliant conclusion. Within
a month from the start from Mashonaland the Salisbury and
Victoria citizens had beaten back the Matabele in two engagements and had occupied Bulawayo, and, although this success
was marred by the unfortunate massacre of the patrol under
Allan Wilson at the Shangani River, the Matabele campaign
will for all time stand out as one of the most notable exploits
in which British irregular troops have ever been engaged.

CHAPTER VI.

GOLD.

"WHAT about the gold?" I hear someone say: "What about Monomotapa, King Solomon's Mines, the land of Ophir, and all the other romantic legends which were in men's mouths before the Pioneers marched up to Mashonaland?"

Fantastic as some of these stories were, there were undoubtedly men, otherwise sane, in that company of adventurers who expected to see quartz-reefs studded with lumps of gold all ready to be chipped off, and to be able to dip wash-dirt out of the river beds with the certainty of finding nuggets in every bucketful. And who shall blame them? I possess a well-thumbed copy of a book by Thomas Baines, the companion of Livingstone and almost the first Englishman to explore Mashonaland. It was given to me by one of the senior officers of the Pioneers, who had it with him during the expedition, and he, or perhaps someone to whom he lent it, scored with heavy pencil-marks several passages relating to the richness of the gold-fields. Here is one for instance, in which Baines quotes the report of a German geologist—Carl Mauch—on the country between the Queque and Bembesi rivers :—"There," he says, "the extent and beauty of the gold-fields are such that I stood as it were transfixed, and for a few minutes was unable to use the hammer. Thousands of persons might work on this extensive gold-field without interfering with one another."

There was plenty more in the same strain, all calculated to create the most exaggerated anticipations of the wealth awaiting those who were first in the field.

And certain evidence which the Pioneers came upon during their northward march was distinctly encouraging. When the column reached the high-veld, permission was given to some of its members to verify the accounts of the ruins of Zimbabwe which were reported to be situated in the neighbourhood of Fort Victoria. Rumours of these ruins had first reached Europe in the sixteenth century through the Portuguese, who had sent several expeditions to occupy the East coast of Africa and had tried on many occasions to pene-

Zimbabwe—Entrance to Elliptical Temple

trate inland. It is probable that none of them actually reached Zimbabwe, but from native sources they gleaned particulars which enabled them to give a fairly accurate description of the stone city and to pronounce it to be the capital of Monomotapa whose " Emperor " held sway over a vast tract of the interior of Africa. In the middle of the nineteenth century, the ruins were actually visited by several bold explorers, including the aforesaid German, Mauch, and detailed descriptions were published, which gave rise to speculative theories as to the people who had built them and the strange rites practised at the central temple.

The party from the Pioneer column reached the ruins without difficulty, and, though forest trees and the dense undergrowth of ages made any close survey impossible, they saw enough to realise that their extent and importance had not been overstated. Before them stood the elliptical temple with massive walls built up of countless evenly-shaped blocks of granite fitted together without the aid of mortar, and so closely that the blade of a knife could not be inserted at the joints. Before them also were the cone-shaped towers, altars, dark passages and curious monoliths described by previous visitors, while the adjacent hills were terraced with an elaborate system of stone ramparts and observation posts, whose construction showed them to be the handiwork of a race far higher in the scale of civilisation than any modern African natives. Here then, on the very threshold of the promised land, was substantial proof that part of the old legends was founded on fact, and if part why not the whole ?

A few weeks later, when the column reached its goal and its members were released for independent prospecting, they found further evidence which gave a significant clue to the occupation of the former inhabitants of Monomotapa. For when they examined the gold belts they found pits and shallow excavations, and in some cases shafts with heaps of quartz dumped near their mouths as if ready for treatment—perhaps by fire. At some time or other it was clear that the land had been seething with industry, and that a vast population had been engaged there in the search for gold, for wherever a promising formation was to be found, there they had left their trail.

But who could they have been ? Certainly not natives of the type of the existing Mashonas who possessed no gold ornaments, and, though skilful workers in iron, seemed to have no interest in the more precious metal, except that here and there one found individuals carrying on a desultory trade in quills containing gold dust and minute nuggets obtained from the alluvial deposits in the river beds.

And why had these ancient miners mysteriously disappeared ? Could it have been—the thought was rather a disturbing one—that, having picked out the eyes of the country, they had found it not worth while to remain and had packed up and taken their departure ?

Whoever they were they had been thoroughly expert prospectors, and their successors, the Pioneers, who were amateurs with no special knowledge of geology, found that the easiest way to locate gold-bearing reefs was to bribe a local native—generally by the gift of a cotton blanket—to guide them to a " hole " or old working. In this way most of the Rhodesian gold mines were started. In fact, so little that was of value had been overlooked by the ancients that even at the present day the cases where mining has been commenced on a virgin reef can be counted on one's fingers.

The absolute ownership of all gold, precious stones and other minerals in Mashonaland was claimed by the Chartered Company, which was also, of course, the Government. Its title was not challenged, for everybody knew about the mineral concession which Rhodes' agents, Messrs. Rudd, Maguire and Thompson, had obtained from Lobengula, the Matabele king, two or there years before, and which had received the blessing of Her Majesty's Government. Nor did anyone question the right of Lobengula to grant these exclusive privileges over an immense tract of country in which no single member of his tribe had ever resided and which to the bloodthirsty Matabele was simply a convenient hunting ground where they could annually pursue their favourite diversions of chasing and spearing the inoffensive villagers, burning the old women and abducting the younger ones.

An English lawyer might say that if anybody had a right to the minerals it was the local Mashona Chiefs, who were in most cases the lineal representatives of dynasties dating back to the ancient kingdom of Monomotapa. But among savage African tribes " rights " are meaningless abstractions unless kept alive by force, and these local natives stood in such terror of Lobengula's raiding armies that they never would have dared to assert their independence. Be that as it may, Lobengula himself had no doubt that he was the absolute sovereign over the people and the land and all that lay below the surface, and drove an exceedingly hard bargain in disposing of the last. It never occurred to him that, in selling to white men the right to dig for gold and other minerals in Mashonaland, he was striking a blow at the national institution of raiding, which followed a regular programme and had become an annual fixture, and it was because of his failure to grasp this fact that he eventually came into collision with the British settlers.

The Chartered Company themselves took no risks, and hedged round their mineral rights with rules which to-day would be regarded as somewhat arbitrary. Before anyone could obtain a licence to prospect—before, indeed, he could enter the Territory —he was required to sign an undertaking " to comply with all the laws and regulations of the Company, to assist in the defence of Mashonaland or in the maintenance of public order when called upon to do so, and to obey without question all the decisions and directions of the Company's officers, subject to forfeiture of thi' licence." The undertaking concluded with these words : " An' I acknowledge the right of the Company to remove me from the sphere of their operations if I resist such decisions or disobey such directions." A Mussolini could not have gone further than this, but when it is remembered that in those days all territory outside the recognised boundaries of the two British Colonies and the two Boer republics was regarded more or less as no man's land, and that several attempts had already been made by Boer filibusters and others to set up independent governments in adjacent native districts, the Company can hardly be blamed for demanding unequivocal submission from anyone who wanted to take advantage of the opportunities offered by them, and no well-intentioned settler cavilled at these terms, which, it was recognised, were aimed, not at law-abiding citizens, but at the reckless and undisciplined freebooters who in the early 'nineties infested the frontiers of South African colonies. Equally justifiable was the provision that the person who pegged out gold claims could not sit on them and wait, but must do a certain amount of development work—fixed in the first instance at a shaft at least thirty feet in depth—within a specified time, in order to secure his holding. But another of the Company's regulations was regarded with suspicion by the diggers and open hostility by investors. It was that known as " the fifty per cent. clause," under which all reef claims were, from the very beginning, held by the digger on joint account in equal shares with the Chartered Company, which, though it spent no money on development, thus enjoyed the position of a sleeping partner. If the digger wished to float his property into a syndicate or joint-stock company, the Charter had first to be consulted, and in any case became entitled to half the vendor's scrip upon flotation. This remarkable principle emanated from Rhodes himself, whose idea was that the Charter should waive all the licences which in most mining countries were paid by the digger during the development stage, and in lieu thereof should retain a half interest in the property itself. Rhodes at the outset often expressed satisfaction at the originality of the idea. He even saw humour in it, and chuckled when he tried to justify it at early meetings of the Chartered shareholders. " We have not had the slightest difficulty," he told them when he first referred to it, " in settling with the various corporations who have obtained capital from the public. The great objection to the idea is its newness. It had never been tried before. It has now been tried and accepted, for a very simple reason. The prospector has found that he is not eaten up by monthly licences while holding his claim ; the capitalist, when he goes to purchase, knows that the Charter has a certain interest, and pays accordingly ; and as to the public, who always find the capital for quartz mining, it is a matter of no importance to them whether Jones gets all the vendor scrip, or whether Jones and the Charter share it together."

There was an element of sophistry here. In practice the fifty per cent. clause led to many abuses, chief of which was that in order to provide the Charter with the requisite share interest the companies formed to carry on gold-mining were over-capitalised. The diggers themselves never shook off the uneasy suspicion that half the proceeds of their properties went into the greedy maw of the Charter ; and eventually Rhodes and his colleagues decided to abandon the principle and to substitute a system of royalties.

When I reached Salisbury in 1891 the first feverish expectations had cooled down, but, nevertheless, gold still formed the uppermost interest of all the pioneers and of the new prospecting syndicates, whose expeditions were beginning to arrive daily.

In Salisbury it was a common sight to see a group of spectators gathered round somebody who was " panning a sample "—that is, shaking a shallow iron dish containing pounded quartz mixed with water, and gradually washing away the lighter sands until only the heavy metallic contents were left. If there was gold it finally showed itself at the bottom of the pan—sometimes a good thick streak, but more often merely a " colour " or a " trace." The " Camp " was kept in a constant ferment by reports of discoveries of new reefs sparkling with gold, and there was a constant coming and going of diggers and prospectors who claimed to have " struck it rich." If you met an acquaintance or got into conversation with a stranger, he was pretty certain after a few minutes' talk to draw you aside mysteriously, and, diving his hand into his pocket, to produce a small chunk of quartz, the surface of which he would lick in order to bring out clearly the specks of " visible." Sometimes these waistcoat-pocket speci- mens actually contained more gold than quartz ; but in any case the confidential disclosure was always the prelude to an offer to allow you as a special favour to participate for a trivial considera- tion in the pleasant task of developing a valuable discovery— of becoming, in short, the joint owner of a gold mine.

The very first time such an invitation came my way I succumbed. I went, indeed, further, and introduced the tempter—a weatherbeaten prospector, by name Barberton Joe, who assured me that he had stumbled on the richest reef in Mashonaland, carrying eight ounces of gold to the ton—to a couple of friends, who, after inspecting the samples, agreed with me that it would be sheer madness to let slip the opportunity of making a rapid fortune. We then and there formed ourselves into a partnership, which we called " The Southern Cross Syndicate," Joe agreeing to become the working member, bringing his professional experience into the firm and carrying out the field work, while the rest of us were to provide the funds. It cost us £60 to equip him with the necessary drills, picks and dynamite, food for himself and trade goods to pay the wages of a few natives whom he undertook to engage, and four pack donkeys to convey all this paraphernalia to the site of the wonderful discovery. But what was £60 compared with the wealth that was dangled before our eyes? Then, after a few days, we got word that he had secured four blocks on the eight-ounce reef, and our excitement rose to fever-heat. We felt that our fortunes were as good as made.

In order to comply with the regulations the next step was to sink a shaft, and Joe, having got together some raw natives, started at once with drills and dynamite. After sinking a few feet he rigged up a rough wooden windlass with a rope and bucket by which he and his workers could be lowered into the hole, and at first all went well.

Joe's knowledge of native languages was extremely limited. For intercourse with his windlass boys he was restricted to two words. When working in the shaft if he wanted to be lowered he used the word " panzi "—the Kaffir equivalent of " down " ; and when he wished to be hauled to the surface he would call out " pezulu," meaning "up." Having sunk his shaft down to about forty feet he had the bad luck to strike an underground spring which made further work impossible without a pump, but before coming into Salisbury to report this difficulty he resolved to test the depth of the water, and for this purpose made a final descent into the hole. At thirty feet his toes touched the water and he decided to give up further investigation and to signal to the windlass boys to haul him up. Unfortunately he became a little flustered and called out the wrong word, " panzi," whereat they obediently lowered him. " Panzi ! " he cried frantically as the water lapped his legs, and down he went again until the water reached his neck. With a despairing effort he gave a final yell " panzi ! " At this stage one of the windlass boys leant over the mouth of the shaft and shouted out *Ikona futi tambu baas !* ("we've come to the end of the rope, Sir") and the situation was saved.

If we had stuck to these claims we might have made a good round sum out of them, for they were situated on an extension of the well-known " Jumbo " reef and were afterwards included in a flotation for, I think, £40,000. But alas! we were impatient. We thought it tame work sitting on our property and never seeing any results, and when, simultaneously with the water trouble, we heard the exciting news of a fresh and far richer discovery in another direction, we lost our heads and actually paid £1 a block for the right to withdraw our pegs so that we might be free to use our licences on the fresh strike. Long before we could prove its value our funds were exhausted, the Southern Cross Syndicate was dissolved and Barberton Joe took his services elsewhere. This was my first and last experience as a " mine-owner."

The professional prospector led a hard life. When on the move he was fortunate if he had as much as a bell-tent to shield him from the weather and from the attacks of mosquitoes and other insect pests, and even when he had located his claims and started working he was seldom able to provide better shelter than a rough grass hut scratched together by the natives, with a flimsy fence of brushwood to keep out beasts of prey. Ignorant of the modern precautions against malaria he was often down with fever, and if, as frequently happened, his native boys then deserted, he was left to fight it out alone, for he was invariably out of reach of doctors or hospitals. To eke out his scanty rations of tea and sugar he had to depend on his gun, and when his day's work was over he had no resources except perhaps a tattered novel or an ancient magazine. (One poor devil, it was said, had nothing to enliven his solitude for three weeks but an old copy of " Bradshaw.") If he had a companion there was certainly less monotony, but the hard conditions were not

Ikona futi Fambu baas !

calculated to cement a friendship, and most prospectors preferred to work alone. Some excuse must therefore be made for the " outbreak " in which he occasionally indulged on return to a town, especially when he had succeeded in realising a sum of money by sale of part of his interest in his mining property or as payment for a contract. There were always plenty of friends to help him to dissipate his earnings at the nearest canteen, where his long abstinence was apt to break down under the combined effects of unwonted society and an abundance of bad liquor.

When the native rebellion burst unexpectedly upon the country in 1896 dozens of prospectors were caught either singly or in parties of two or three and ruthlessly butchered on their claims by the wretched Mashonas whom they had till then regarded with supreme contempt. In most cases their pitiful fate was made certain by the discovery on the veld of their battered and often mutilated remains, but there were a few who disappeared as completely as if they had been drowned at sea, and whose end could only be guessed. A favourite device of the rebels was to drop the bodies of their victims into a shaft and fling burning brushwood after them to obliterate all traces of the crime. In one instance a prospector, by name O'Connor, was suddenly attacked by his own workers and forced to take refuge in his shaft. The natives then tried to smoke him out with burning faggots, and finally to blow him to pieces with charges of dynamite, but by some miracle he escaped death from the explosions and when the coast was clear succeeded in making his way, badly scorched and severely wounded, to Bulawayo where he was gradually nursed back to health—only to be struck dead by lightning a few months later !

The use of dynamite by natives on this occasion was exceptional. In the early days before the rebellion they were horribly afraid of explosives and always nervous when charges were being fired. This part of the operation was, of course, never entrusted to native mine-workers for fear of accidents, and prudent miners were careful to count the shots and to examine the rock carefully if there was any suspicion of a misfire. In other respects, however, they were not always so cautious and it was a common practice among white miners to leave unsupervised boys in charge of the windlass while they went below to place the dynamite in position and prepare the shots for firing. This carelessness nearly caused the death of Bill Upsher, a well-known prospector who had lost all his hair and was in the habit of wearing a rich brown wig. He had descended into his shaft alone to fire some charges, and, finding the heat rather trying when he got below, had removed his wig and placed it in his pocket. Having set three or four sticks of dynamite in position, primed them, and lighted the time fuses, he signalled to the two boys on the surface to wind him up. All went well until he was close to the top, when the natives, who were expecting to see their master with his fine head of abundant glossy hair, were astonished at the spectacle of a bald unfamiliar cranium slowly emerging from the bowels of the earth. One of them yelled out " Umtagati ! " (The Devil !) and the pair of them instantly let go the crank handles and fled precipitately, leaving poor Bill Upsher to hurtle down to the bottom of the shaft, where his dynamite charges were on the verge of exploding. With marvellous presence of mind, considering that he was knocked nearly senseless by the shock of his descent, he whipped out his clasp-knife and cut the fuses. Had he delayed a moment he would have been hoisted into eternity by a far more rapid process than that provided by his windlass. From that day onwards Bill Upsher was never known to wear his unlucky wig.

A haughty aloofness

CHAPTER VII.

Boys.

In Rhodesia the term "boys" means grown-up natives who work for white people, the younger ones being known as "piccanins." Time was when without any contemptuous implication we used to speak of all Bantu people (whether in their own *kraals* or in employment) as "niggers," but we have become so timidly delicate of speech that I fear I should shock refined ears if I used that good old word to-day. So I will call them "boys," and, keeping clear of thorny racial problems, will try and picture the part they played in the life of the early Rhodesian community.

From the very beginning we found a wide difference between the aborigines of the country and the boys from other parts of Africa who came up with the Pioneers or drifted in later from neighbouring territories in search of jobs. The local natives had no stomach for work and treated our arrival with a haughty aloofness. On the other hand, until the rebellion of 1896 brought home to the Government and the settlers the need of some definite policy for their control and the regulation of their movements and mode of living, I cannot say that the early white population of Mashonaland took much interest in their black neighbours. There were, of course, the missionaries, who founded churches and schools in the outside districts; taught their flocks to read and sing hymns; mildly preached the advantage of settled occupation to the men and the impropriety of wearing no clothes to the women, and were rather prone to take their part in real or fancied grievances against the white folk. The intentions of these good men were in every way praiseworthy, but they were generally looked at askance, for the popular impression was that they laid too much emphasis on the "man-and-brother" theory, and overlooked the necessity for starting at the bottom and gradually inculcating ideas of discipline, hygiene and thrift, with the result that the black man was led to regard himself as the equal of the white and became uppish and troublesome. I hasten to add that Christian missions are now conducted in a far broader and more enlight-

45

ened spirit, and that the prejudice against them has in consequence practically disappeared.

Then there were the traders who visited the kraals, and made a living by bartering calico, old uniforms, beads, salt, brass wire and other European trade stuff coveted by the natives, for Kaffir corn, mealies and cattle. But, putting these two classes aside, the ordinary man was only concerned in obtaining cooks or waggon boys or labourers for his farm or claims, and in none of these capacities were the indigenous Mashona of any value. At first the idea of working at all for white men was utterly strange to them. In their natural state, and in their own primitive and inefficient way, they were cattle-breeders and tillers of the soil, and one might have thought that they would have taken kindly to farm work for wages ; but it was not so. Nor were they attracted by house-work, in spite of the opportunities which it presented for picking up discarded clothes, empty tins and bottles and other odds and ends. For a long time they appeared unable to rid themselves of the suspicion that underneath the sudden irruption of white men there lay some sinister design against themselves, and even if, greatly daring, a boy engaged himself to wash up the dishes or sweep out the hut of the *Mlungu*, he was almost certain to decamp as soon as he had achieved the adventure of a month's service.

Then again it took a long time for a savage, unused to tableware, brushes and crockery, and satisfied in his own home with one or two bowls or platters for every kind of viand, to grasp the different uses of the multitude of strange utensils and appliances with which even the most frugal Englishman surrounds himself—to realise that a sock, though admirably adapted for the purpose, should not be employed as a coffee strainer, and that it is an offence against good taste to clean out the inside of a saucepan with his master's hair-brush.

For domestic purposes, therefore, we relied mainly on boys imported from the territories on the East Coast, where they had long been accustomed to work for slothful Portuguese employers, and had become fairly efficient house servants. Miners and farmers, however, were engaged in a constant struggle to obtain labour from a class to whom regular employment was an utterly unfamiliar idea, and who found a month's wages sufficient to satisfy their requirements for the remainder of the year. The local natives had not yet learnt to value the things that money would buy. Their vanity was tickled by wearing European garments, but they could generally acquire cast-off jackets and trousers without paying for them. They had not at first any inducement to earn money for taxation, for the hut tax was not introduced during the first two or three years after the Occupation. In fact, in his natural state, and before artificial wants grew in his mind, the male Mashona had only two needs—food and wives. His grain, sweet potatoes, ground-nuts and other crops were mainly produced by the labour of the women. The more agreeable duty of snaring birds, rats and other small game, or of driving antelopes and larger animals into prepared pits, or catching locusts and hunting for caterpillars—for nothing came amiss to the native menu—was the man's part. To obtain his first wife he had to acquire cattle, but, as a girl was usually betrothed in her infancy, her fiancé had plenty of time to accumulate the four or five head which was the customary price demanded by her father. Once married, his great ambition was to beget daughters whom he could in turn bestow in matrimony, and, with the cattle obtained for them, buy more wives to work for him and keep him in idleness. Such, in his primitive state, and before white men intruded with their ceaseless activities and demands for more and more labour, was the cycle of the Mashona man's life, and the only means by which he could be weaned from this idyllic existence was the creation of a desire for European manufactured goods purchasable with money. His modern standard of luxury, which prompts him to buy new clothes, concertinas, gramophones and bicycles, was a very gradual growth undreamed of in the 'nineties.

The early Rhodesian settlers were unconscious of this economic process, and concentrated their efforts on coaxing boys to come and work and on keeping them as long as possible by decent treatment and regular wages. Few gave heed to the customs and lore of the tribes around them, whom they loosely and incorrectly lumped together as " Mashona "—a garbled form of of *Amazwina*, " the dirty ones," which was the contemptuous nickname bestowed on them by their oppressors the Matabele. Nevertheless, although much of it is veiled in obscurity, these Mashona possess a long and most interesting history, for in the constant ebb and flow of movement which for centuries has been at work among the Bantu races of South Central Africa, they seem to have acquired more permanence of habitat and tradition than most of their neighbours. Among themselves they are still the *Makalanga*—" the people of the Sun "—whose ancestors, bearing that name, speaking the same language, and ruled by dynastic chiefs with the same titles, were there when the Portuguese arrived in East Africa in the early 16th century. True, when we first came in contact with them they were cowed and abject from the ever-present dread of Matabele raids, but in spite of this they retained a spark of the pride of race. Asked to what tribe they belonged they would respond *Tiri wanu,* " We are men." Here and there were individuals with something distinctive—almost aristocratic—in their appearance ; with olive skins, and the thin lips and aquiline features of an Arab—irresistibly suggesting a " throw-back " to ancestors among the vanished people who had left those other legacies of ruined stone temples and abandoned gold mines. Such arts and crafts as weaving, basket-making and working in iron were more highly developed in the Mashona than in most other African tribes, and there were traces among them of an ancient cult, manifested in curious and significant practices whose meaning and origin they were unable to explain. Their implements, for example, frequently bore evidence of a form of sex-worship. The earthenware furnaces in which they smelted iron were rudely modelled to imitate a woman's trunk and legs, the upper part being decorated with mouldings of the two breasts and navel, and indented marks corresponding to the pattern with which women tattooed their stomachs—differing for each tribal division. Similar designs, sometimes more, sometimes less conventionalised, were carved on their wooden war-drums, on the head rests which served as pillows and on other articles of common use, and it was a custom in some districts to reproduce the breasts, navel and tattoo marks in the clay forming the interior walls of dwelling huts. Practices connected with witchcraft were highly developed among all the Mashona, their wizards enjoying a reputation for occult powers which caused them to be consulted by neighbouring tribes, including even the Matabele, who in other respects treated them with supreme contempt.

Of all this we knew nothing and cared less. We saw comparatively little of the local natives in Salisbury, for, although there were several kraals within a few miles of the fort, their occupants were at first too timid to come in and seek work, and only ventured to approach in parties of a dozen or so to offer their wretched produce for barter, invariably leaving the township before nightfall. On such occasions the meal and other goods for sale were loaded on to the women, who bore them on their heads in great baskets, most of them having babies as well swaddled in leather aprons on their backs. (A Kaffir woman always has a baby. As soon as one is weaned another takes its place.) The men strutted in front, each equipped with a regular armoury of weapons—a murderous-looking battle axe with two or three assegais and a knobkerrie,

Mashona woman going to market

or occasionally a bow and a sheaf of arrows. Sometimes there would be one—generally a petty chief—carrying an antiquated firearm. These "family guns," as we called them, were flint-locks ranging from the genuine bell-mouthed blunderbuss to the muzzle-loading "Brown Bess" of Crimean days; they were obtained from early traders, carefully treasured, and handed down from father to son. No attempt was made by the authorities at that time to prevent the Mashona from going about armed, for no one dreamt of their daring to make use of their weapons against the white men. Guns, so far as we could judge, they only carried for effect, like small boys playing at soldiers. They certainly were exceedingly shy of discharging them. They used home-made powder composed, I think, of charcoal and nitre, and for bullets anything which came handy in the way of small stones, short lengths of wire, or nails. (During the rebel-lion of 1896 there were cases of horrid wounds inflicted at short range by the glass balls taken out of old-fashioned soda-water bottles.) Once, when travelling with my family, we met a party of armed natives on the road, and bribed one of them, who carried a Tower musket with its stock elaborately bound round with brass and copper wire, to let off a charge. With evident reluct-ance and only after enlisting the support of two of his friends, he braced himself for the effort and pulled the trigger. There was a hissing noise in the barrel as the powder gradually ignited. Then, with a tremendous bang, out burst a shower of gravel and an immense cloud of black smoke. Simultaneously, the gun gave a desperate kick causing the owner to reel, while the others shouted with excitement at his intrepid act. For a long time afterwards they discussed this unprecedented event, going through the whole business in pantomime over and over again.

My wife wanted to buy a bow and arrows as curios, and, while bargaining with the owner, fitted an arrow into the bow and pretended to aim it at him. He gave a yell of terror and instantly the whole party, armed as they were to the teeth, scattered in a panic, only stopping when they had put themselves, as they thought, safely out of range. When they turned and saw our amusement they roared with laughter at the excellent joke and chaffed the bow man and each other without the slightest sign of abashment.

One would hardly have thought that such arrant cowards would be capable of attack, and yet these were the very natives who, egged on by their wizards, were guilty, a few months later, of the simultaneous murder of over a hundred white men and women whom they caught unawares and butchered in cold blood.

Almost all the tribes of Rhodesia, but especially the Mashona, possess the uncanny faculty of communicating news over great distances within an incredibly short space of time. All sorts of theories have been hazarded as to the process by which this " bush telegraphy " is carried on. Some believe that the natives transmit signals by means of their war-drums. But, if this is the case, the code employed must be of a very unusual nature, for nothing can be more monotonous to the uninitiated ear than the rhythmical tom-toming which is often kept up at Kaffir kraals half-way through the night. A more satisfactory explanation is that at every village there is a sort of official town-crier whose business it is to mount to the summit of a rock and broadcast the tidings of any notable event. Villages within earshot pick up the calls and at once pass them on, and within a few minutes they are relayed far and wide. I have had ocular demonstrations of this practice on several occasions and can testify that the shouting from kraal to kraal actually takes place, but I am convinced that some more subtle agency, and one which is beyond the present comprehension of Europeans, is utilised. Whatever be the explanation, it is certain that natives receive information of events occurring at a great distance far more rapidly than white men with their telephones and telegraphs. The news of the disaster which overtook Allan Wilson's patrol at Shangani in December, 1893, was current among natives working in Salisbury—more than two hundred miles away—many hours in advance of the first official messages, and weeks before the details of the massacre were known. During the early stages of the Boer War people at Bulawayo heard reports of several critical engagements— Spion Kop, for one—from native sources within a few hours of their occurrence, although the scene of action was five or six hundred miles off, and anyone who has lived in native districts could supply other authentic examples of the speed with which news is disseminated among the blacks.

Trading native produce was a laborious process, but one in which the natives themselves positively revelled. They would only sell their goods in driblets and, as time was of no consequence to them, were ready to spend hours in haggling over each item. I remember an encounter with an old woman who carried a basket apparently containing nothing but meal. Squatting on the veld, with this between her knees, she burrowed for a while and extracted a minute egg, which she offered in exchange for beads. Quite five minutes were expended in securing this prize, the beads being keenly scrutinised and discussed with her friends, who all took an interested part in the proceedings. Eventually, when she found me deaf to her entreaties to add a few more, a bargain was struck, the beads handed over, wrapped up in a rag and safely stowed away in her pouch. At once she dipped again into the meal and produced a second egg and the same process had to be gone through. This was repeated until after about an hour's negotiations I succeeded in buying—one by one—ten eggs, which exhausted her stock.

I have said that the boys who came to us for housework were generally natives of the Portuguese Colonies on the coasts, but there were others from far more distant parts—Zulus from Natal, missionary-trained boys from Blantyre in Nyasaland, and even some from far Uganda—all attracted by the high rates of pay which were based on the South African scale. Most of them had a weakness for European garments and would sacrifice personal comfort in order to appear smartly dressed. Boots, for instance, were worn only for show and were kept for use in towns and native villages, on other occasions being carried in the hand. In later years I had a servant from Kenya belonging to the Kavirondo tribe who in their own country then wore no clothes at all. While at work in my house he had to wear a uniform, but, when going out for a Sunday afternoon's walk, he used to appear in a Baden-Powell hat carefully whitened, a blazer, cord riding breeches, puttees, brown boots and a pair of large swan-necked spurs (generally upside down). To an elegant walking-cane he had screwed a bicycle bell which he sounded frequently as he swaggered along the road, and, thus arrayed, he enjoyed the feeling that the eyes of everyone —the Almighty included—were upon him. Even in the natives' own villages odd articles of civilised attire were in great request, and were often worn detached from their usual accompaniments. Gambo, an important tribal chief under Lobengula and the commander of one of his crack regiments, on ceremonial occasions always donned an old opera hat, and, as his only other garment was the ordinary skin kilt worn by all Matabele, the effect was decidedly *chic*.

The zeal of the missionary-trained boys, who generally had a fair knowledge of English, led sometimes to embarrassing situations. Of course, in the very early days there were no white women and such social amenities as " calls " were unknown, but when a few wives and sisters came up the English

practice was gradually introduced. One had accordingly to be
on one's guard against the houseboy's tendency, in the absence
of his mistress, to show indiscriminate cordiality towards all
and sundry in the way of casual callers—even to the extent of
offering them refreshment. As door-bells were unknown, it
was a common plan for married ladies to place on the *stoep* a
tray for cards, together with a little frame with the words
"At Home" and "Not at Home," either of which could be
displayed by a sliding arrangement for the information of
visitors. A new-comer sent her houseboy, a missionary product
who spoke fair English, down to the general store to get one of
these appliances and explained carefully what she wanted and
its purpose. The boy professed to understand and went off,
full of importance, to execute his commission. Imagine the
feelings of his mistress when he returned later in the day with a
cardboard box containing a small brass apparatus for attachment
to a door, with a sliding bolt by means of which the words
" Vacant " or " Engaged " could be made to appear at will !

The Chartered Company prohibited the sale or gift of liquor
to natives under the most severe penalties, and the tribes of the
country have in consequence remained uncontaminated by
drink, which has had such a demoralising effect upon the coloured
populations of other parts of Africa. The Cape Colony boys
and many of those from Portuguese territory, debarred from
freely purchasing the spirit to which they were accustomed,
were full of devices for obtaining it by illicit means, and those
who worked in private houses, of course, had opportunities of
stealing it. A Goanese cook employed by one of the Police
messes was suspected of helping himself and accordingly a decoy
bottle of sherry standing on a sideboard was liberally doctored
with jalap. At dinner that evening after the officers had par-
taken of soup someone called attention to the bottle in which the
wine had fallen three or four inches below the level of the previous
day. The Mess President summoned the Goanese, and sternly
accused him. " Antonio, you black devil, you've been at the
sherry ! " " No, sah," he protested, " me no drink master's
sherry, me put um in master's soup ! "

In the old settled districts of Cape Colony, the Free State
and the Transvaal conversation between white people and their
servants was usually carried on in a wretched *patois* based on
Cape Dutch, while in the native districts, where tribes of pure-
bred Bantu stock survived, farmers and others were usually
able to talk to them in their own tongue. But in Mashonaland
it was different. The white people were suddenly pitchforked

into a country where the more familiar dialects of the Zulus, Basutos and Xosas were useless. Common necessity and the aptitude of the natives themselves led to a compromise, and the strange and elastic language known as " Kitchen Kaffir " came into being. It consisted of a few English, Dutch and Kaffir words strung together in a feeble imitation of Kaffir phraseology. New words were added as occasion demanded, or as they were picked up by white men from the native speech, and *vice versa*, while a certain amount of expressive pantomime was generally introduced into a conversation. Thus a master discussing wages with a boy, having grasped the fact that the word for " ten " in some dialect or other was *shumi*, and remembering that native plurals often began with *ma*—would hold up the fingers of both hands and say *mashilling mashumi*—obviously " ten shillings." The boys did their best to respond by giving their own queer version of English words, such as *imbokisi* for " box," *isteema* (steamer) for " engine," and *istolo* for " store." The chief merit of this jargon was that it pleased both parties—the boy, who thought he was talking in English, and the master, who fondly imagined himself a Kaffir linguist.

Most of the boys employed in farms, houses and stables were supplied with idiotic English names, and took a pride in them. One whose real name might be " Indafunia," or something equally melodious, would cheerfully answer to " Lobster " or " Monkey." Such names had a piquant flavour when used in official documents. I once saw a magistrate's *subpœna*, which opened in the following way : " VICTORIA, by the Grace of God, Queen, Defender of the Faith, unto JACKASS, Greeting, etc." The boys, on their side, coined nicknames for their masters which they used in private conversation among themselves, and were rather loth to disclose, but which generally bore allusion to some peculiarity of habits or appearance and were often very apt. A well-known Native Commissioner, remarkable for the size of his feet, was dubbed *Manyatela* (boots) ; a clerk who used a typewriter *Mtiki-tiki*, and a man who wore glasses *Mechlomana* (four-eyes).

Although the imported boys whom we used as house-servants were astonishingly quick and observant, they often sprung a surprise upon us by misdirected efforts arising from an excess of zeal and anxiety to do the right thing.

A Salisbury lady, who had picked a few flowers in her garden and stuck them carelessly and temporarily into her bedroom water-jug, was astonished a day or two later, when she had some friends to lunch, to find the same jug planted in the middle of the table with a large bunch of potatoes in flower arranged in it. Such little pleasantries were harmless, and gave a certain spice to housekeeping which never grew stale, because one never could be quite sure what one's boy would do next.

Taking them as a whole, our native boys were a merry, cheerful and willing lot. They were always trying to learn, and responded heartily to good treatment. Many a time after our return to England, when struggling with the details of insurance cards, or trying to follow the etiquette of " afternoons out," or taking up the references of prospective cooks, we heaved a sigh of regret for the simplicity of the domestic problem in Rhodesia. There, if one wanted, say, a kitchen boy, one would tell the cook to let his friends know. In due course a nondescript would arrive, and say *Funa sebenza* (" I want work "). He would produce his " pass," showing his recent employers and the wages they had paid him, and tell you his name was " Sixpence," or " Pumpkin," or something equally insignificant, and that he wanted *ipondo mabili* (£2) a month. Scornfully you would offer him 15s., and your other servants would back you up by enlarging on the advantages and comfort of employment in the household of so generous a master. To the accompaniment of much chaff a bargain would be struck at £1, and there and then he would begin work and stick to it—at any rate until the first month was up, when, if satisfied, he would carry on indefinitely. No trouble about a separate bedroom or evenings out. He would shake down in the " boys' compound " with the others—a crowded hut being what a native enjoys most, especially on a cold night— while from time to time he would ask for a few hours' freedom, the invariable excuse being a desire to visit *bloola ga meena* (" my brother "). If he felt the need of an occasional restorative he would report sick for the sole purpose of gratifying his passion for white man's *muti* (medicine). Asked to indicate the seat of trouble he would point with melancholy resignation to his stomach or his head. A liberal dose of Epsom salts in the one case, or quinine, in the other, would send him away completely satisfied. At one time an employer, when parting with a servant, was allowed to write a character on his pass, but the practice was open to abuse, and if a boy found out from some friend able to read that he was carrying about an unfavourable testimonial he would " lose " the pass and obtain a fresh one from the Registrar. Nevertheless I remember a boy applying to me for an engagement, and, with complete assurance, exhibiting a pass upon which his late master had written, " This boy resembles the lilies of the field."

A Mashona Family

Before leaving the subject I might mention that the acquisition of an experienced house-boy not only meant an immense increase in one's personal comfort, but carried indirect advantages of a social character. When people took to giving dinner parties I am sure that I frequently owed hospitality—not to any endearing qualities of my own, but to the fact that I was the happy possessor of a " butler " whose table manners were the envy of all my friends. Many a time a letter inviting me to a dinner party has contained a postscript such as this : " Would you be so kind as to bring Alfred with you to help our boys "—a request that I cheerfully complied with, as it meant that I, at all events, would be well looked after.

CHAPTER VIII.

Coach and Rail.

RHODESIA's earliest and most serious handicap was one of geography; her greatest triumph that she conquered it. When Rhodes started on his scheme of colonisation, Mashonaland was the most difficult country to get into—or out of— in the whole Empire. What hope was there of progress with the nearest utilisable sea-port 1,600 miles away and a weary wagon journey of three months between the new gold-fields and the terminus of the railway? But Rhodes had persuaded some hundreds of his fellow-countrymen to go there, and had induced some thousands of British investors to put up the money to help them stay there, and unless he could bring machinery to enable them to work the gold and find an outlet for their crops and produce, his whole enterprise would be damned as a supreme failure. So he shouldered the immense task of extending the Cape Railway system across the desolate waste of Bechuanaland to the frontiers of the newly-opened territory, and simultaneously made arrangements to run a light line of 2-foot gauge rapidly up from the Portuguese Coast towards Umtali and Salisbury. In both cases the contracts were entrusted to a firm of engineers mainly composed of members of one family—the Paulings—at whose head stood George Pauling, one of the boldest railway builders that Great Britain has produced; a man after Rhodes' heart; one who said he would " get there "—*and got there*. Into the methods by which Rhodes financed these two railways it is not necessary to enter, beyond mentioning that not one penny of the cost fell upon either the British taxpayers or the Rhodesian settlers.

During the construction of the trunk line from the south, goods continued to be carried over a gradually shortening road-journey by ox-waggon, and passengers and mails by a regular service of coaches on the American model. The development of the coach service produced another outstanding figure— a young Colonial of Boer extraction, by name Christian Zeederberg, known to all his friends—and they were innumerable— as " Doul." He was a man of splendid physique and untiring energy. His somewhat unintelligent countenance masked a

56

Early type of Rhodesian Coach

Zeederburg's Coach crossing Blinkwater Spruit

natural shrewdness which enabled him not only to get the best work out of his employees, white and coloured, but to make some extremely lucrative contracts with the Chartered Company, and when he died—a comparatively young man—he had amassed a respectable fortune. It was related that after the Matabele war, when a contract for a mail-coach service between Bulawayo and Salisbury was under consideration, Jameson at first wanted a tri-weekly service and offered him a substantial Government subsidy if he would undertake it. Doul replied that his resources in mules and rolling stock were not equal to this, but he was prepared to provide a *bi-weekly* service for two-thirds of the price. This seemed to Jameson a fair compromise and the agreement was concluded by an exchange of letters. It was only after the bargain had been struck that Jameson discovered that, whereas " tri-weekly " meant three times a week, " bi-weekly " meant once a fortnight. Doul had already made sure of this by looking up the words in a dictionary.

Doul's kindly disposition won him a host of friends, among whom was Rhodes himself. During the secondary stage of the Boer War, Lord Roberts was marching on Pretoria and President Kruger was gradually preparing for his final and sensational exit by removing his headquarters (but not his wife, who remained at Pretoria) to successive points on the line to Delagoa Bay. At this time Rhodes was in Bulawayo, and one night, discussing the situation at a dinner party at Government House, he expressed the view that the old President had no intention of deserting the Transvaal, but that as soon as he was driven back to the Portuguese border he would surrender to the British forces. Doul Zeederberg, who was one of Rhodes' guests that evening, dissented. He was sure that Kruger was in a panic and meant to make a bolt, and he said so. At this Rhodes became quite vehement, and elaborated an imaginary conversation which, he said, Oom Paul must have had with Mrs. Kruger just before leaving Pretoria. " You, my dear, will stay here at home, and you will be quite safe, for even if the Englishmen do reach Pretoria they will not molest a woman. I will slip away eastward for a while while my burghers are driving them back. But if the Almighty wills it that the *verdomde rooinekes* overtake me, I shall give myself up and then they will bring me back to you. . . ." and so on.

Doul thought this over for a minute, and then said, " Why Mr. Rhodes, anybody would think you had been under the bed listening ! " There was a roar of laughter in which Rhodes

himself joined, and eventually he offered to bet £25 that he
would be proved right. This was what Doul wanted. He
took up the wager at once, and a few weeks later, when the
news came that the old President had got safely away from
Delagoa Bay, he claimed his money.

One more anecdote, which Doul Zeederberg was fond of
telling against himself, relates to his well-known habit of rising
at grey dawn—" sparrow-chirp " as he called it—to attend to
business. He had been on a mild spree in Bulawayo and did
not return to his home till about two o'clock in the morning.
Anxious to avoid disturbing his sleeping household he began
to disrobe in the dining room, but unfortunately let one of his
boots drop on the floor. The noise roused his better half,
who got out of bed and came to the door, when, seeing her
husband partially dressed, she enquired why he was *getting up*
at that unearthly hour. " One of the mules is sick," he replied,
" and I must see to it," and thereupon, with grim resignation,
he reclothed himself and left the house to spend the remainder
of the night in uneasy slumber on some bundles of forage in
the stable.

I have said enough in a previous chapter about the misery
of African coach-travelling. In Rhodesia it was aggravated
in the rainy season when the lumbering vehicles were apt to
be held up for many hours by swollen and unfordable rivers.
Fortunate were the passengers if the stoppage occurred near
one of the wayside stores which were dotted along the route,
for they could at least get a cup of tea, and a tin of sardines
and perhaps some cookies, to keep them from starving. But
tinned foods at wayside stores were a risky diet. A friend
of mine who had outspanned one evening at the Umzingwani
drift, went to the store to replenish his commissariat and bought
a couple of tins of " bully beef " from the Jew proprietor. When
he came to open them for supper at his waggon he found to
his disgust that the contents of both tins were mouldy and
bad. Indignantly he tramped back to the store and displayed
them to the Jew. " Look at it, you skellum ! " he said. " Why
the meat is actually blue ! " " Very sorry, Sir," replied the
trembling storekeeper, " but I don't stock no other colour."

In one respect the Rhodesian coach service afforded a strong
contrast to conditions in the pioneer days of California and
Australia. Valuable consignments of gold coin and boxes of
smelted bullion from the mines were frequently carried in the
mail bags, and the coaches had long stretches of wild and unin-
habited country to traverse. There was never a military escort,

and it would have been a comparatively easy matter for two or three determined men on horseback to hold up the coach and rifle the mails, especially on the eastern side of Mashonaland, where robbers would have had little difficulty in slipping with their booty into Portuguese territory and gaining security from arrest. Yet in the whole period from 1893 to 1902, when a through connection by railway was established, no such attempt was ever made.

The building of the railway line from Vryburg to Matabeleland was a fine feet of engineering, but was not on the whole marked by any very outstanding events. Something like a record, however, was achieved on the section of 500 miles between Mafeking and Bulawayo. When the native rebellion broke out in March, 1896, the railhead was still at Mafeking, and all troops sent up for the relief of the harassed population of Matabeleland had to move by road. The position was greatly complicated by the epidemic of rinderpest which, in a few weeks, swept all ox-transport out of existence and left nothing but rotting carcasses at the outspans and along the track. Construction began at Mafeking in April, 1896, and by October of the following year the rails reached Bulawayo, the work having been pushed forward at the rate of about a mile a day. The arrival of the railway at the place which only four years before had been the principal military town of that wonderful old savage, Lobengula, the last King of the Matabele, was marked by a carnival of festivity at which many distinguished men from England and from other parts of South Africa were present by invitation of the Chartered Company, and an opportunity was given to the Hon. Arthur Lawley, the deputy-Administrator, such as rarely occurs to young men at the opening of their career. He had the responsibility of presiding at the official functions and of making several important speeches, and he magnetised all present by his unexpected gift of oratory. From that moment he was a marked man and from a position of comparative obscurity rose rapidly to one important post after another, until finally he was appointed to the Governorship of one of the provinces of India.

If there was little romance about the Western line, the building of the Beira Railway was accompanied by a full measure of adventure and interest. Beira, now a civilised port, and even a seaside resort for Mashonalanders in winter time, was in those days by far the most depressing of the wretched Portuguese settlements on the East coast of Africa. A few sickly-looking Bunniahs and Goanese half-breeds carried on a feeble trade in miserable shanties of corrugated iron ; a few undersized soldiers kept up a pretence of garrison duty, which consisted mainly in blowing bugles at all hours of the day, and a sprinkling of Swahilis and Zambesi natives hung about to discharge the cargoes of the small coasting steamers from Zanzibar or Lourenço Marques that occasionally called at the port. The only structures that could by courtesy be termed " buildings " were the Governor's bungalow, the British Vice-Consulate, and a one-storied hotel, " The Royal," kept by a cheerful and hospitable Italian by name Martini, of whom many old Rhodesians will have pleasant recollections. Leading up from the quay was a dreadful highway of deep loose quicksand to walk along which was a penance. Immediately in rear of the sand-spit—for that was all Beira really was—lay a fetid swamp, the breeding-place of voracious mosquitoes. At nightfall these descended in thousands on the jaded inhabitants, who were all more or less sodden with malaria. The Pungwe and Busi rivers, whose estuaries combined to form the harbour, brought down enormous quantities of silt which grew into shifting banks, rendering navigation treacherous and difficult for all but small steamers, but the bar which is found at the mouths of most African rivers was absent.

Before the railway works started the *Venice*, the *Norseman* and the *Induna*, small coasters of the Union and Rennie lines, paid more or less regular calls with passengers and cargo from Durban and Delagoa Bay, but my first arrival was in a dirty little vessel belonging to the German East Africa line which I chiefly remember for her rats and cockroaches, and for the reek of copra which clung to her from her last cargo. There were half-a-dozen cabins, one of which I shared with a prospector from the Rand, named Cunningham, and at the end of the alley way were two bathrooms, one labelled *Damen-bad*, and the other simply *Bad*. Knowing something of German habits I got up early to make sure of the first bath. But Cunningham had been before me. " Take my tip," he said, " and go to the one on the port-side. Although it's marked ' Damn bad,' it's a long way cleaner than the other."

The railway construction did not start from Beira but from a point 30 or 40 miles up the river Pungwe, where a small township grew up—Fontesvilla of unhallowed memory. Passengers for up-country reached this point in a river steamer commanded by a brawny and genial north-country man, Captain Dickie, who had lost two fingers of his right hand from blood-poisoning caused by punching a nigger in the mouth. In addition to

At Fontesvilla 1894.   s.s. Kimberley at anchor

navigating the vessel he used to provide food and liquor for the
voyage (which seldom occupied less than 20 hours), and found
this a highly profitable business. He knew the river and its
shoals and sand-banks as an Oxford waterman knows the Isis
between Folly Bridge and Iffley, and when the passengers did
their duty by the good things provided for them he brought
them up to Fontesvilla with admirable punctuality. Accidents
only occurred when the supply of whiskey was in excess of the
demand. In such cases it was noted that the *Kimberley* was
wont to get stranded on a sand-bank about five miles below
Fontesvilla and that all efforts to re-float her were useless until
Captain Dickie's whiskey had been consumed. Coincidences
of this kind were not likely to escape the attention of Cecil
Rhodes, who, on the single occasion when he made the trip,
inquired of Dickie before starting how much whiskey he had
provided. " Two cases, Mr. Rhodes," said Dickie, " and a case
of champagne. You needn't be afraid of running short."
" Well," said the great man, " how much will you take for the
lot ? " Dickie at once grasped the situation and a broad smile
overspread his sun-baked countenance. Eventually a bargain
was struck. Rhodes bought the entire stock for £25, and the
Kimberley, relieved of any responsibility, made the passage in
12 hours, beating all previous records.

In spite of its pleasant name, which suggests cooling streams
and suburban amenities, Fontesvilla was a loathly little camp
in the old construction days and had a most unsavoury reputation both on account of its unhealthiness and by reason of the
human riff-raff—Dagos, half-bred Portuguese and the like—
which had been attracted there. Insufferably hot and seething
with malaria it had, during its palmy days, probably the highest
death-rate of any place in the world. In the wet season it was
liable to sudden inundations from the muddy water of the Pungwe
River, and on this account the houses—even the tiny Roman
Catholic Church—were built on piles. It was difficult even to
bury the dead decently, for a few feet below the surface of the
ground one came on water, and heavy weights had to be placed
on the coffins to keep them down until the graves were filled in
with soil.

In the enervating climate of the Pungwe flats and the entire
absence of any form of social amusement, it was not surprising
that there was a good deal of drinking. It seemed as if this
was the only thing to do. But, although drunken brawls were
not unknown, there was on the whole very little serious crime.
For that the credit was due to the engineer in charge of the

construction—Mr. A. L. Lawley, and his English assistants, who kept a tight hand on the sub-contractors and their employees and did not hesitate to exercise control over the numerous loafers of mixed nationalities who hung about the railway camps. Had the maintenance of order depended on the Portuguese police and other officials who were in nominal authority, the state of affairs, at Fontesvilla especially, would have been very different, for there were some pretty shady characters knocking about. The only attempt at bloodshed that I ever personally witnessed took place in the so-called hotel and was started by a dispute between a newly-landed English passenger (who, by the way, bore a historical name) and the villainous-looking off-coloured barman, who had tried to cheat him over the change for a sovereign which the former had tendered for some drinks. The barman used insulting language, and the Englishman, rather foolishly perhaps, " plugged " him in the eye. Instantly there was a general melée in the crowded saloon and I espied two or three of the queer customers drawing their knives. The Englishman stood a chance of being very roughly handled, but somebody knocked out the light and in the confusion which followed we managed to rush him out into the open air.

The passenger who to-day travels from Salisbury to Beira in a few hours, and finds the heat oppressive and the flies a nuisance, can have very little conception of the trying conditions under which that little two-foot-gauge railway line was pushed up into the interior in 1892 and 1893. The first stretch of forty or fifty miles offered no physical difficulties, as the country was as flat as a pancake, and the work consisted mainly of banking the permanent way to a sufficient height to keep the rails from being washed away in the summer floods. Nevertheless, this section was the one which exacted the heaviest toll of sickness and death. For one thing, the heat was terrific. The Pungwe flats are only a few feet above sea level ; the vegetation consists of long grass broken by occasional clumps of palms, but otherwise destitute of shade. In 1892 immense herds of buffaloes, zebras, wildebeeste and other large game roamed over the flats, and lions were a perfect scourge. Following the game came the vicious tsetse fly—not then recognised as dangerous to human beings, but capable of inflicting painful stings. But the most insidious pest was the mosquito, which, although no one knew it at the time, was responsible for the virulent malaria which afflicted practically every white man engaged on the railway works. So deadly was the combined effect of heat and fever that the engine-drivers and other railway workers had to be duplicated in order to ensure continuous reliefs. I shall always remember the first time I passed through Fontesvilla on my way to the coast, because of a tragi-comic series of incidents which took place while I was waiting for the *Kimberley*, which, as usual, had run aground on the Bigamiti sandbank. Mr. Lawley, with his usual hospitality, put me up for the night at his comfortable bungalow—the one oasis in that abominable camp. While we were sitting at dinner the sound of a woman's screams reached us, and at the same moment a note was handed to my host informing him that one of his most capable engine-drivers had just died of blackwater fever. A coffin having been hastily knocked together out of packing-case wood, the unfortunate man's remains were placed in it and deposited for the night in the Roman Catholic Church. Early the following morning we went to attend the funeral, and waited outside with the widow (who was still giving vent to her grief with loud lamentation) while half-a-dozen fellow-workers of the deceased went in to bring out the coffin. A moment later they all emerged in a hurry, beating their heads and swearing, and informed us that a swarm of wild bees had settled on the bier, and would let no one approach it. They retired to the canteen opposite the church, held a council of war and fortified themselves for a second attempt. But again they were baffled, and forced to beat a retreat without effecting their purpose. Finally a squad of boys was got together and promised a big reward if they would tackle the job. They made a rush, secured the coffin, and brought it out safely at the double, but the bees came too, and the whole funeral party, widow included, was forced to proceed at a jog-trot to the cemetery, beating off the maddened insects as they went, and getting not a few stings on the way.

The bereaved lady had since the previous evening kept up a continuous wailing, which harrowed everyone's nerves to such an extent that they hastily raised a subscription of £100 or so to get her away. She left for the coast by the *Kimberley* the same afternoon, and at Beira caught the steamer by which I was travelling. When we reached Durban, five days later, she appeared to have recovered her spirits. I spoke a few words of condolence to her, and was rather startled when she told me that she had already become engaged to one of the ship's stokers !

It was very seldom that a padre could be found to perform the rites of burial over the victims of malaria, and this duty generally fell to the lot of one of the engineers of the construction party, or the medical officer, if he happened to be on the spot. The latter officiated once at such a ceremony, when the sad proceedings were relieved by a touch of human comedy. A platelayer had died, leaving behind him a devoted chum, who, although much overcome, busied himself in making preparations for the funeral, assuaging his grief at frequent intervals by the solace of the whiskey bottle. By evening, when he joined the little group of engineers, platelayers and gangers assembled at the graveside the poor fellow was fairly drunk, but he remained alive to his responsibilities as chief mourner, and took advantage of the pause when the body was being lowered to address the doctor in an alcoholic but audible whisper : " You quite understand, Dr. Williams, sir," he murmured, " on this occasion all drinksh are at my expensh."

When the line was nearing completion George Pauling himself came up to Chimoio and spent some days in overhauling the construction staff. Several redundant Europeans were paid off and discharged and other economies effected. The gangers and platelayers and employees generally were a good deal perturbed, for retrenchment was the order of the day, and no one knew whose turn was coming next. A white man came to the contractor's office and craved an interview. He was admitted, and stood patiently waiting, hat in hand, till Mr. Pauling was ready to attend to him. At last he looked up from his writing:

" Well, what do you want to see me about ? "

" If you, please, sir, I'm Dickson, who was ganger at the 45-mile peg, and you gave me the sack yesterday."

" Well, you got a month's pay, didn't you ? "

" Oh yes, sir ; it isn't that ; but I hope my being sacked won't affect my brother's prospects ? "

" Your brother ? What part of the line is he working on ? "

" Oh, he ain't on this line ; he's working in Canada. But seeing as how you appear to have bought the b—— world, I was afraid he might lose his job too ! "

CHAPTER IX.

JUSTICE.

" JUSTICE, Freedom, Commerce "—such was the impressive, if rather smug, motto adopted by the Chartered Company. The interpretation of these watchwords by the light-hearted young men who rallied round Rhodes and Jameson in the " jolly-dog " era was refreshingly casual, but they were taken in sober earnest by those who controlled the destinies of the new colony. Incidentally, they were printed under the coat of arms at the head of the Company's notepaper, where they may have had a slightly misleading effect, for a clerk in the Civil Service once received a private letter addressed to him in a feminine hand, " A. B., Esq., care of Messrs. Justice, Freedom & Commerce," which suggested that he had been using official paper for his love-letters.

" Justice," in the long run, means " Fair play," and in that sense was given ungrudgingly by the Company, though the British Government, in deference to what was then called the " Exeter Hall " sentiment, took a narrower view and allowed a certain suspicion to peep out in their attitude towards the whole enterprise. They were certainly not enamoured of it. It was Rhodes' importunity thát prevailed on them to grant the charter in the first instance, and the despatches written by members of the Cabinet at the time prove that the inducement that weighed with them was the opportunity of getting the credit of a policy of Imperial expansion with as little worry as possible and, above all, without expense. But they were not going to allow themselves to be effaced entirely from the picture, and accordingly they instructed the High Commissioner at the Cape to exercise a general control over the Company, and, when occupation was accomplished and Rhodes was ready to start on ·the work of administration, they asserted the right to be consulted as to the appointment of judicial officers for the new territories.

The legal machinery instituted by Jameson, with the sanction of the Crown, was something like the primitive windlasses and dollies used for the extraction of gold before batteries and hauling gear could be imported—it had to be adapted from the material ready to hand. So it came about that half a dozen young officers, with no more experience of judicial practice than they had acquired in the orderly-room, suddenly found themselves appointed Resident Magistrates, responsible, among other things, for " paying careful regard to the customs and laws of the class or tribe or nation . . . especially with respect to the holding possession, transfer and disposition of lands and goods and testate and intestate succession thereto and marriage, divorce and legitimacy. . . ." to quote the resounding text of the charter. Small wonder if freakish decisions were sometimes given. What is creditable is that the horse sense, characteristic of British Army officers transplanted into alien surroundings, prevented any injustice either to white men or natives. Jameson gave his magistrates a free hand, but he was not blind to the need for making his courts of justice conform outwardly to those of the older Colonies, and he discreetly imported a clever young lawyer from the south to play the part of mentor both for himself and his subordinates, in legal matters. This was Mr. Alfred Caldecott, who had already made his mark at Kimberley by carrying out the complicated legal business necessitated by the amalgamation of the diamond mines. His nominal post was that of Public Prosecutor, but he really exercised, on a magnified scale, the benevolent supervision which an English magistrate's clerk employs to keep his bench of J.P.s within due bounds. He did this with tact and good humour, and with great benefit to all concerned, until, three years later, he died prematurely of blackwater fever.

Only a week before his death he appeared in my court— I was then R.M. of Salisbury—to prosecute a hotel keeper for permitting gambling on his licensed premises, and about a dozen well-known citizens, who had been found there playing cards when the police broke in, for " aiding and abetting." The game was baccarat and Caldecott displayed an expert knowledge of it which quite overwhelmed the law-agent retained for the defence. What puzzled me, however, was the unusual hilarity in the crowded court-house while Caldecott was making an impassioned denunciation of the evils of gambling in general and the special enormity of baccarat. The explanation came when the case was over and we were riding home together. " Weren't you surprised," he said, " to find what a lot I knew about baccarat ? " " Yes," I replied, " frankly, I was. But why was everybody laughing at you ? " " Well," he said, " you were probably the only person in court who didn't know that I was playing baccarat there myself that very evening.

Jack Spreckley

But I happened to have left the room when the police raided it ! "

The Public Prosecutor could not, of course, always be present in court, and the magistrates were generally left to conduct cases —both civil and criminal—by the light of their own common-sense. Captain Wallace, magistrate of one of the smaller town-ships, once heard a civil dispute, with a long string of witnesses whose evidence occupied the whole morning. In the end he gave judgment for the plaintiff. The smart law-agent who was for the other side jumped up and said, " Your Worship, I give notice of appeal." "Very well," remarked Wallace, in a weary voice, "but it's a quarter-to-one now and time for tiffin, so I'll try the appeal to-morrow morning."

In the more-important districts the Government was repre-sented by a Civil Commissioner. Sometimes the same official was appointed C.C. and R.M., but where the offices were held separately the C.C. was the senior and the " big pot " of the district. Nevertheless the police took their orders from the R.M. On the first Christmas Day after his appoint-ment as R.M., our friend Wallace, who had been celebrating the occasion, fell foul of the C.C., a somewhat dour Scotch-man, who was so provoked that he suspended him from duty. A little later, on returning to his quarters, the C.C. was confronted by a couple of police under a sergeant who informed him that he had orders from Captain Wallace to place him under arrest. And arrested he was. But the humour of this little escapade was lost on the authorities, who decided that Wallace's ideas of judicial practice were too advanced, and allowed him to retire into private life.

Another of the pioneer magistrates in the Jamesonian period was Jack Spreckley, a jolly, impetuous young fellow with an irresistible tendency to practical joking. His first appointment was at Lomagunda, a lonely station some three days' journey on horseback from Salisbury. When he had been there only a month or so he sent a native runner with a chit to Dr. Jameson, applying for a week's Christmas leave which he proposed to spend in Salisbury. The application only reached the Doctor on Christmas Eve and he at once sent the native back with a letter refusing the leave. He was rather taken aback, however, when, about ten minutes later, Spreckley himself strolled into the office. " What the devil are you doing away from your station ? " he asked, with some heat. " Well, sir," replied Jack, quite unmoved, " as I've had no answer to my letter, I thought the ave was all right, so I came in."

Spreckley, who did some gallant work in the Matabele War, afterwards left the Civil Service and joined Willoughby's Company, which, among other activities, obtained a concession to supply water to the new township of Bulawayo. A big dam or reservoir was constructed a few miles out of town and Spreckley was placed in charge of the operations. When the rainy season began he was instructed to cable daily to the London board the amount of water in the dam, and for some days the directors were greatly pleased at his messages reporting progress. " Three feet of water in dam," " Five feet of water in dam," " Ten feet of water in dam." This was highly encouraging and they published the cablegrams and congratulated themselves on the fat profits which the new waterworks would shortly bring in. But their hopes were dashed by Spreckley's next cablegram, which was short and to the point, " Dam bust."

Behind his gaiety of heart Spreckley possessed great pluck and the capacity for leading men. His life was cut short by a Boer bullet while he was leading a squadron of Rhodesia Horse at an engagement in the Transvaal during the South African War.

One of the functions of a Magistrate was to act as marriage officer, but for this he had to have a separate commission. The Hon. Harry White, another occupant of the bench, failed to grasp this, and within the first few months of his appointment united several couples in what they innocently regarded as the bonds of matrimony. As White had not received the necessary powers, the marriages were held to be invalid, and the delicate position in which the parties were placed had to be rectified by a proclamation of the High Commissioner. It was rumoured that one at least of those whom the Magistrate had joined together evinced no anxiety for the relief to be applied to his own case.

Sometimes the marriage ceremony was accompanied by piquant incidents. I once officiated at the wedding of a well-known bruiser with a lady whose main profession was that of barmaid at one of the canteens. They were a popular couple and quite a number of their friends attended the nuptials. Next morning on arrival at the Court-house, I found the happy pair, the best man and bridesmaid, all somewhat the worse for wear—the leading lady had a black eye—waiting to answer a charge of being drunk and assaulting the police, two members of the force being also in attendance whose battered appearance was an eloquent testimony to the allegation. But there was no sign of rancour on either side, and, when it transpired that both the policemen had themselves been wedding guests, I felt that the interests of justice would be served by a few words of caution. These were listened to with polite attention by the bride and bridegroom, while their discharge was received by their many friends in Court with rapturous applause (immediately suppressed).

The oddest case that I had to do with was that of a Boer transport-rider, whom I will call Grobler—an elderly widower, who presented himself to be married to a very young girl obviously below the prescribed age. She blushingly admitted that she was only 17, and, as her father lived in Natal, the ceremony had to be postponed for his written consent, which was not forthcoming for three or four weeks. This obstacle surmounted, the pair once more applied, but in the meantime I had ascertained that Grobler had several minor children in the Orange Free State, and according to Roman-Dutch law, which was in force in Rhodesia, I should have to satisfy myself, before marrying him, that he had made pro-vision by deed for their education and maintenance. So the unlucky couple were once more disappointed. Weeks rolled by, and I had forgotten all about them, when one morning they again turned up in excellent spirits—the lady, I fancied, somewhat more mature in appearance. The deed of " Kinderbewys " was triumphantly produced and was found to be in order ; the usual interrogatories about prohibited degrees and so forth were put and satisfactorily answered on oath by both parties, and the knot was tied. That very afternoon I met a friend who asked me, " Is it true you married old Grobler and his girl this morning ? " " Yes," I said, with a certain misgiving, " What about it ? " " Well," my friend said, " You've done it this time. You've married him to his own niece ! " It was perfectly correct, but Mr. and Mrs. Grobler had already left Salisbury on their way down country, and I hadn't the heart to issue a warrant for their arrest for making a false affidavit, so I held my peace. The solution of the problem was a melancholy one, for less than a month later the native rebellion broke out and Grobler was one of the first victims.

Magistrates were also required to hold inquests, and these were of fairly frequent occurrence, mainly, I think, because the police received a special fee for attendance at them, and were thereby stimulated to unusual exertions to find subjects for inquiry. The Assistant Magistrate of Salisbury, Mr. George Farmaner, on the first day of his appointment, was called upon to sit in judgment on some " human " remains which had been collected on the veld by a zealous policeman, or perhaps by some boy engaged for the purpose. They consisted of a skull (of some antiquity and clearly the former property of a native), an old jacket and a rusty revolver. The connection between the three relics was not particularly obvious and no medical evidence was called, but that did not discourage Farmaner who mastered the problem without hesitation, and pronounced a verdict of " Suicide whilst in a state of temporary insanity."

This faculty of disentangling legal puzzles was one in which Farmaner excelled, and was enlivened by the artistic phraseology in which he delivered his judgments. A complicated cross-summons for assault, in which two leading residents were involved and much hard swearing was indulged in by the partisans on both sides, was disposed of by him with a discretion worthy of King Solomon. " I shall cut the Georgian knot," he said, " by finding you both ' not guilty,' and I'll tell you for why. I've come to the conclusion that you both provocated one another." To an intimate friend he afterwards gave additional reasons for his decision : " You see, I was there when the row began and I advised them to settle it with their fists. But that, of course, is strictly *inter alia*, so you mustn't repeat it."

No one could complain in Rhodesia of the law's delays. Early in 1893, an atrocious crime was committed near Salisbury by a Zulu boy who ran amuck and shot dead a man, a woman and her child, all white people, besides wounding the woman's husband so seriously that he died later. The murderer at first got away, but not for long. Within 48 hours he was traced to the native compound at Salisbury, arrested, and brought before the magistrate. Four days later he was tried before Dr. Jameson, sitting as Chief Magistrate with assessors, and sentenced to death, and he would assuredly have been hung within a week of the crime, but for the fact that the sentence had to be confirmed by the High Commissioner. The latter declined to give his decision on the telegraphic statement of the facts sent to him by the Doctor, and insisted on seeing the actual depositions of evidence. In the end the miscreant was executed just six weeks from the date of the crime.

As was invariably the case in Rhodesia, this tragedy had its humorous accompaniment. When the first news of the murders reached Salisbury, public opinion ran very high, and on the evening of the Zulu's arrest a number of excited citizens made an attempt to lynch him. Headed by a fiery little baker who had provided himself with a length of manilla rope, they made a rush for the police station, but the sergeant had got

Salisbury Gaol in 1892

Early Rhodesian Architecture

wind of their intention, and under cover of the darkness had
smuggled the wretched man away to the gaol, whither the
lynchers next betook themselves. In the meantime Jameson
had been apprised of the ferment, and, galloping on horse-back
to the scene, found some fifty of them on the point of breaking
into the flimsy building. " Gentlemen ! " he cried, without
dismounting, " I ask you to pause. Remember that the country
is on the eve of a boom. For God's sake don't do anything
to stop it ! " This entirely irrelevant argument caused the
party to hesitate, and when the Doctor invited them to come
across to the Masonic Hotel, and talk the matter over quietly,
the crisis was over. A round or two of drinks, and an assurance
by the Doctor that justice should take its course, clinched the
matter, and, after singing " For he's a jolly good fellow " and
" God save the Queen," the lynchers dispersed. The sequel
came a few days later when a bill was sent to the Government
by the baker for fifteen shillings for the rope which he alleged that
the Doctor had made off with in the confusion of the moment !

In arresting this Zulu luck favoured the authorities, for if
he had kept clear of Salisbury he could have hidden himself
indefinitely in native kraals, where it would have been next
to impossible to trace him. But a white criminal would have
had great difficulty in getting clear away, and, although several
attempts of this sort were made, I can recall only one that was
successful. While a gang of hard-labour convicts was repairing
the street in the middle of Salisbury, Mr. Deary, a leading
merchant, rode up to his store, threw his reins over a rail and
left the horse standing while he went inside to transact some
business. One of the white convicts made a dash for the horse,
mounted, and before the startled guards could recover their
presence of mind or level their rifles had galloped off across
the veld. At a farm a few miles out of Salisbury he found
some clothes hanging up to dry on a line, which enabled him to
discard his prison garb. Further on he met a farmer whom he
persuaded to buy the horse, and then set out to tramp to the
Zambesi. He ultimately made his way to Fort Jameson in
Northern Rhodesia, where he was identified and detained. But
nobody wanted him back in Mashonaland, least of all the Doctor,
who reflected that the cost of sending a police escort round
by sea and up the Zambesi and Shire rivers to fetch him would
have run into some hundreds of pounds, and therefore declined
to take any steps to recover him. The authorities in Northern
Rhodesia, therefore, had no alternative but to release him, and,
as they also were reluctant to bear the expense of deporting him,

they had to give him a Government job. He was a clever rascal, and when I last heard of him he had changed his name and was practising as a medical man, but of course he gave Mashonaland a wide berth.

The position of white convicts in Salisbury—there were never more than three or four—was in those days more humiliating than it would be in England or even at the Cape. Practically the only way of keeping them occupied was to employ them on road-making or similar work in and about the town, where, in such a small community, they were of course recognised by the " man in the street." As a set-off against this, their life within the gaol walls was made as tolerable as possible by liberal food and by privileges, such as tobacco, which are not usually allowed to hard-labour prisoners. It is related of one long-sentence man, whose conduct was so good that he was sent out daily to do carpentry jobs without a guard, that he was seen one evening running down the street with his bag of tools on his shoulder by a friend who wanted him to stop and have a chat. " Can't wait ! " he shouted as he hurried past. " The gaol shuts at six, and if I don't get back in time I'll be locked out."

Like everything else in the earlies, the maintenance of law and order was in the hands of amateurs, but what they lacked in experience they made up for by zeal. The Rhodesian police force from the very beginning had the reputation of being one of the finest semi-military corps in the Empire, and competition to join it was, especially in the pioneer days, very keen. Many of the best settlers in the Colony served an apprenticeship in its ranks. Originally it was largely recruited from what was known as the " public school " type, and contained quite a number of younger sons of good English families, leavened by a sprinkling of warrant and non-commissioned officers drafted in from the regular army. Of the latter one of the best known was the late William Bodle, an ex-cavalry sergeant, who joined the old Chartered Company's police in 1890 as R.S.M., and, after serving with much distinction in every campaign within his reach, rose eventually to command the force. He retired on pension several years before the Great War, but volunteered again for active service in 1914, went out to France and was promoted to the rank of Brigadier-General. Among scores of similar figures my mind goes back to Sergeant-major " Jimmy " Blatherwick, a famous riding-school instructor with a splendid flow of good-natured sarcasm. You would have had to get up very early to corner Jimmy. Calling the roll of a new batch of recruits one morning, he came on an unfamiliar name which he pronounced " Montaig." As there was no " Here, Sir ! " in response, he glanced up and down the squad and spotted his man. " Why don't you answer when I call out your name ? " he rapped out. " You haven't called my name, Sergeant-major," replied the innocent. " Oh, haven't I ? What *is* your name ? " " Montague, Sir." " Montigew, is it ? Very well, Trooper Montigew, you'll report for *fatigew* at 10 o'clock."

A good deal of the detective work of the police was done by the " Black Watch," a trained corps of natives acting under white supervision. We found them extremely useful in Mashonaland during and immediately after the rebellion. In fact, without their aid we should never have succeeded in tracking down the ring-leaders and those guilty of the brutal murders which were perpetrated round Salisbury in the dark days of June, 1896. As it was, many of the worst rebels went scot-free for lack of evidence to convict them. One notorious wretch for whom we had long been scouring the country was at last rounded up by the Black Watch in the Charter district. Although there was some circumstantial evidence, the case against him rested mainly on the testimony of a single native, who, for fear lest he should be intimidated or put out of the way, was kept in custody at Fort Charter. When the criminal was actually arrested, he and the witness were sent on foot to Salisbury in charge of an escort of three of the native police, who for greater security handcuffed their two charges together. On the road the accused man tried to make a bolt, dragging the witness—perhaps not entirely against his will—with him. They succeeded in getting about fifty yards away, when the police-corporal fired, and shot dead—the witness ! Of course the case against the real culprit had to be abandoned.

CHAPTER X.

Freedom and Commerce.

WHAT the founders of the Chartered Company had in mind when they made " Freedom " their second watchword I cannot pretend to say. Indeed, until I began to write this chapter I never gave the subject a thought. Probably there was some idea of trumpeting their intention of abolishing slavery, but in Mashonaland, on which they concentrated their first endeavours, there was no slavery in the accepted sense of the word. Certainly the natives there were infamously treated by their ruthless neighbours the Matabele, who regarded them much in the same light as they did antelope and other game— that is, as their lawful prey, to be rounded up and slaughtered periodically for amusement and profit. But the Mashona boys and girls, whose lives they generally spared, were not sold as slaves. They were adopted into the tribe, and treated with no greater harshness than the young of the Matabele themselves.

" Freedom," however, in the wider sense, was a striking feature of our own life in those first years, before Town Councils and Legislative Assemblies had come into existence to make laws and regulations for our welfare and improvement, and before social restrictions began to undermine our liberties. Outside the rather haphazard businesses of prospecting for gold, which was a form of gambling, and farming, which at first meant only cutting down trees and selling the wood, or cultivating a small patch of mealies, we were mainly engaged in the primitive satisfaction of our creature wants. Problems of food and housing occupied us far more than abstract questions of government, political rights, or the development of the country. We were rather like a shipwrecked party on a vast island, abundantly supplied with natural resources, but unhampered by the burdens of civilisation. Few of us in those times recognised what lucky dogs we were. Our only cares were the minor inconveniences of living at the back of beyond—a temporary shortage of coffee, perhaps, or candles, or soap or some such commodity not really essential to existence ; or a delay in the arrival of the English mail, or the collapse of one's hut, which was a small matter, after all, as one could build another in three days.

In the matter of dress there was a delightful freedom from convention. The standard costume was a grey flannel shirt, a pair of khaki " slacks " and a " smasher " hat. In 1892, when a few women drifted up-country, the store keepers imported reach-me-down suits, and the young bloods began to preen themselves, trim their beards, and don collars and neck-ties, but for a long time I can recall only one person who wore—or even possessed—a coat, and he probably thought it was due to the dignity of his office to do so. That was the Bishop of Mashonaland—not the first, Dr. Knight-Bruce, of whom we saw next to nothing, but his successor, Dr. Gaul—still, I am happy to say, alive and hale in South Africa—who used to describe himself as the smallest Bishop with the largest diocese in Christendom. He was rather a dressy little man, and went to the length of appearing in a khaki drill apron in addition to a clerical coat of the same colour and material. The outward badges of episcopal rank he was quite prepared to doff in an emergency, as a rough miner, who once travelled with him on the coach, discovered. This worthy had been making himself objectionable to his fellow-passengers and using offensive language, and at one of the halts Dr. Gaul warned him that if he did not behave himself he would be turned off the coach. " Who's going to turn me off ? " demanded the miner. " Not you ! If you wasn't a sky-pilot, I'd knock the stuffing out of you ! " Quick as lightning the Bishop (whose early training on the diamond fields had taught him how to take care of himself) divested himself of coat and apron, which he threw on the ground, rolled his shirt-sleeves to the elbows, and squared up to his man. " There's the Bishop of Mashonaland," he said, pointing to the discarded garments, " and here's Billy Gaul ! Now, come on ! "

Few of the early settlers owned a change of clothes, and in the rainy season it was the custom to carry regulation waterproof ground-sheets, of which, for some reason, there was an inexhaustible supply for sale at the Company's stores. With the aid of a piece of string passed through the eyelet holes these made a fairly efficient substitute for mackintoshes. But I once met a poor fellow on the " wallaby " who did not possess such a luxury. Instead he carried an empty paraffin tin. When the rain came on he took off all his clothes and put them in the tin, so that he always had dry raiment to resume when the sun came out.

In our spacious surroundings everything that nature provided was free for all to take. There were no game laws, and outside the townships it was absolutely necessary to shoot in order to keep the pot filled and provide food for one's " boys." Fortunately buck—the word applied to all the many species of antelope—and guinea fowl, partridges and pheasants were to be found in plenty throughout the country, and a Martini rifle and a shot-gun were part of the normal equipment of every prospector and trader. Some of them added hunting to their regular professions. With a two-wheeled " Scotch cart," a few trade goods and a supply of ammunition, they disappeared into the wilds for weeks at a time in pursuit of buck, buffalo and an occasional elephant, bartering the meat at native kraals for grain which they brought into Salisbury for sale as soon as they had secured a cart-load. There were even one or two whose thirst for profitable adventure led them over the border into the Barue country where they found the Portuguese only too willing to enlist their services in expeditions against their native tribes with whom they were frequently at loggerheads.

The housing problem was not one which exercised us unduly—we were free to put up huts where we liked and how we liked. At Salisbury, poles and grass for thatching were cut as required on the commonage surrounding the " camp." After the pioneers first arrived, there was a long delay in settling on a permanent site for the future township, and men began to throw up huts promiscuously on any level spot that was handy. Later, when the township was being surveyed, these squatters claimed vested rights and made a great outcry at the suggestion that they should shift their miserable shacks of wattle and daub. £500 would have sufficed to compensate all handsomely ; but the Company grudged this small sum and weakly consented to lay out the plots to fit the straggled huts. It was a fatal mistake and one that took years to overcome. To-day, Salisbury is an exceedingly attractive city with wide thoroughfares and many handsome buildings, but it suffered for a long time from the disadvantage of having some of its streets adapted to the irregular lines of the scattered pioneer shanties, instead of being planned in rectangular blocks. In Bulawayo and later townships the mistake was avoided ; the sites were carefully chosen and streets and avenues laid out in squares on the American system.

The site of the little town of Umtali, near the Eastern boundary of the Colony, was shifted because its first position was in mountainous country and difficult of access by the railway from Beira. To save the cost of constructing the line through the hills, Rhodes, with characteristic boldness, decided to move the town to a more approachable spot seven miles away. Those who had purchased building plots in the old township were granted corresponding positions in the new, while Rhodes bought their buildings and sold them to a party of American missionaries. New Umtali was intentionally placed close up to the Anglo-Portuguese boundary, and after the move was made it was discovered that, by some mistake in the survey, a portion of the block of ground assigned to the Magistrate actually lay within Portuguese territory. An adjustment was made later on, but in the interval an elusive white man, against whom a warrant had been issued for some crime and who had managed to evade arrest and slip over the border, was observed seated on the back fence of the garden where, secure under the protection of a foreign power, he proceeded to eat a hearty meal of bread and cheese in full view of Captain Scott-Turner, the Magistrate, who was powerless to touch him.

If " Freedom " was fairly descriptive of our condition of life in the first years after the occupation of Mashonaland, I am afraid that "Commerce " is rather too grand a word to apply to our elementary business transactions. The commerce of Salisbury, which was for a long time the hub of all the activity in the territory, was in the hands of a few importers who brought up by waggon from the south every kind of commodity for which they expected a demand. The storekeeper who sold picks and spades would also deal in ready-made clothing, cartridges, saddlery, provisions, medicine, trade goods for Kafirs, mealies, crockery and, invariably, whiskey. Those who did not keep general stores called themselves " contractors," and went in for brick-making, cutting and riding fire-wood, well-sinking, grave-digging and any other job that could be done by aid of a waggon and a few tools. Others were " commission agents " who bought and sold claims and farms, acted as auctioneers and generally meddled in everybody's affairs.

Gradually a few trades became specialised. A baker, I think, was the first to strike out an independent line. Prior to his opening business we had to make our bread in our own messes, each member in turn taking duty with the bake-pot. How we survived these amateur efforts I cannot imagine, but I well remember the relief and excitement when we heard that genuine white bread was to be bought at a shop at the Kopje. The baker was followed by a chemist and a butcher or two. The messes formed by the Civil Servants, and, of course, the police, drew meat rations from the Company and all slaughtering was done by the regimental butcher, a rather excitable Irishman. His *modus operandi* was primitive. Each afternoon he went to a convenient spot on the outskirts of the camp and took post with a rifle, while a dozen or so of trek oxen were driven past him by the police herd-boys. Having selected a victim he fired —occasionally with fatal results, but if, as frequently happened, his aim was unsteady he lost his head and blazed at random at the scared beasts, which, of course, stampeded in every direction.

The " place of slaughter " happened to be quite close to the compound containing the huts which served as offices for the Company's staff, and on several occasions stray shots came through the mud walls, so that, when we heard the sound of rapid fire, we always lay flat on our faces till the fusillade died away. But all fun from this source disappeared when a real butcher, with a real humane killer, arrived and took over the duty.

These, of course, were the highways of " commerce." There were many by-ways discovered by the ingenious in pursuit of a livelihood. A favourite means of making money was the " salted horse" gamble. It was popularly supposed that an animal which had recovered from an attack of the scourge known as " horse-sickness " became immune and could be taken without risk into veld where the disease was prevalent. The owner could sell such a horse at about four times the ordinary price if he was prepared to give a written guarantee that it was " salted," i.e., had had the disease, together with an undertaking to refund the purchase price if it died of horse-sickness within a specified time—usually a year. New chums were often deluded into giving £80 or more for a guaranteed horse to somebody who had himself bought it for about £20, and who took care to vanish as soon as he got his money. Some of these " tender feet " from England were a godsend to the slim colonial horse-dealers of whom several plied their trade in Mashonaland in the early days, but few were quite so refreshingly innocent as the greenhorn who was induced by a plausible transport rider to buy a pair of mules *for breeding purposes*.

Even the Boers, who generally had the reputation of being fairly wide awake, were no match for these resourceful traders in horses and livestock. A certain Dr. Robinson had a transaction with a Boer for a number of young cattle, which, after much haggling, he agreed to buy at so much a head. Dr. R. then went off to get the money while the Dutchman retired to his waggon and, with the aid of a popular book of tables, well known as the " Ready Reckoner," figured out the total sum he was to receive. By and by the purchaser returned with a bundle of notes and gold, which, on being counted, fell short of this sum by about £10. An altercation followed and the Boer asserted that he must be right because he had got his figures from the " Ready Reckoner," and produced the volume in support of his claim. Dr. R. picked it up and scrutinised it carefully, looked at the title-page, and then flung the book down contemptuously. " Why, man alive ! " he said, " that's no good ! That's a last year's ' Ready Reckoner ' ! "

He earned his title of " Doctor " from a previous exploit in the Orange Free State, when he was engaged on a trading trip which turned out so unprofitable that he was on the point of returning to Kimberley. He had just reached Boshof, a small town close to the border, when he heard that there was an outbreak of smallpox in the neighbourhood and that the country folk were much perturbed. He at once halted and gave out that he was a medical practitioner with ample supplies of lymph and was prepared to perform vaccination at half-a-crown a head, cash down. The news spread and all the Boers for miles round flocked to his waggon with their wives and families to be operated on. Suspicion was aroused a few days later when the usual after-symptoms failed to develop, but by that time the " medical practitioner " had retreated over the border, taking with him his professional secret and about £25 collected in " vaccination " fees, which amply compensated him for the diminution of his stores by a couple of tins of condensed milk !

Talking of condensed milk reminds me that for the first year or so this was all we could get in the towns, and was even regarded as rather a luxury. Gradually a few of the townspeople acquired for their own purposes native cows traded from the Mashonas—tiny little beasts like Dexters, with a milk output of not more than two or three quarts per day. The first people who kept cows for profit in Salisbury grazed them on the commonage and sent milk to their customers in ordinary whiskey bottles, which thus became the standard measure. Even cows were valued in bottles, and were spoken of as " five-bottle," " ten-bottle," and so on, according to their daily yield. The milk bottles were conveyed from house to house by the native equivalent of a milkman, who carried them in canvas pockets sewn on to a sort of waistcoat which fitted over his shoulders and looked like a ship's life-belt. Some of the early dairymen were not unversed in the dodges which, rightly or wrongly, have always been attributed to this business. The milk given by native cows was naturally very rich, and when one had paid 6d. or 8d. a bottle it was irritating to be supplied with a thin, semi-transparent fluid which hardly altered the colour of the breakfast tea. A friend of mine who used to send his own boy with a bottle to a neighbour for his daily supply thought he had expressed his feelings gracefully when he wrote to her as follows :—

" Dear Mrs. So-and-so,
"In future I will send you *two* bottles every day. Would you kindly put the milk in one and the water in the other, and I will do the mixing myself."

The absence of a bank and the dearth of cash in Salisbury led to a vicious system of credit which clung to us like a blight. I don't think it is too much to say that in the first two years a cash purchase over the counter of a store was absolutely unknown. At the hotels one signed cards, and the proprietors thought themselves fortunate if their patrons settled their accounts monthly. This led to extravagance and debt which few escaped. As a set-off against bad or doubtful accounts, tradesmen were compelled to charge higher prices all round, and customers who tried to pay their way had to bear the burden of the defaulters. The ramifications of the credit system were far reaching, and involved everyone. The English Church padré complained of the difficulty in collecting the I.O.U.s which members of his congregation placed in the offertory bag, but on the whole had little to grumble at, because, in the absence of the standard threepenny bit, no one had the courage to sign his name for less than a shilling.

This credit system and the high rate of transport combined to raise the cost of ordinary goods to a level which made housekeeping a constant nightmare. The following list of prices realised at the morning market at Salisbury is taken from the " Rhodesia Herald " of November, 1892, three or four months after the first bank had been opened and the high rates had begun to drop :—

Eggs, 8/6 per doz.
Fowls, 1/10 each (native fowls about as big as bantams).
Butter, 6/- per lb.
Venison, 4d. per lb.
Lettuces, 1/4 each.
Milk, 1/2 per quart.
Candles, 3/- per lb.
Paraffin, 15/- per gal.
English beer, 32/- per doz. pints.

At the auction sale of Lord Randolph Churchill's surplus stores at Salisbury in September, 1891, I saw ordinary three-star brandy sold at £5 a bottle and whiskey at £50 per case. This sort of thing led to a mad effort on the part of traders and speculators to rush up supplies of liquor, and for some weeks little else was imported. Prices in this particular line dropped in consequence with great rapidity, and the local paper gravely informed the public that the " *cost of living* had fallen to 5/- a bottle."

CHAPTER XI.

WILD BEASTS.

THE entry of the Pioneer column with its long train of waggons, its search-light and other military paraphernalia, probably gave the big game animals of Mashonaland a scare from which they never really recovered. The column was followed by a steady and growing stream of transport, much of it in charge of Boer conductors who continually hunted " for the pot " on either side of the road, and the giraffes, zebras, buffaloes and other interesting animals of which we had heard so much learnt to give the beaten track a wide berth. The dispersal of prospectors and farmers in all directions drove them still further into the wilds, and from 1890 onwards the opportunities of seeing or shooting the larger fauna of the country in the immediate neighbourhood of the new townships and mining settlements rapidly decreased. Even further afield the panorama of immense troops of different kinds of big game grazing and galloping about, as depicted in the illustrations to the books of Gordon Cumming and Cornwallis Harris, and as described by Selous in his fascinating journals of travel and sport, was a thing of the past. Still a number of the more common species of antelope could at first be found within fairly easy reach of Salisbury. In 1891 a small herd of tsessebe was frequently grazing within two or three miles of the Kopje, sometimes coming as close in as the racecourse. A troop of about twenty ostriches haunted the Gwibi flats between Salisbury and Mount Hampden for many years, and two of them—a cock and a hen—survived until 1913, and could be seen almost any day about four miles from the township.

That the descriptions of the old hunters were by no means fantastic or exaggerated it was still possible, in the nineties, to have ocular proof—not in Southern Rhodesia, it is true, but in the neighbouring districts North of the Zambesi and on the Pungwe flats in Portuguese territory, on the way to Beira. Within a day's ride of Kalomo, the first headquarters of the Northern Administration, one could make sure in 1903 of finding roan and sable antelope, Burchell's zebra, wart-hog, eland and hartebeeste, besides innumerable small buck such as oribi and

82

duiker. The swampy country near the Kafue River teemed with pookoo and lechwe ; the North bank of the Zambesi gave cover to impala and buffalo, while hippopotami abounded in the river itself. In later years these last-named were a great nuisance to boating parties above the Victoria Falls, and several fatal accidents occurred through their propensity for charging and upsetting canoes. Consequently the authorities in Northern Rhodesia who were nearest to the river encouraged their destruction. If, however, they chose to stick to the South bank they were safe, for under the laws of Southern Rhodesia they fell within the category of " Royal "—*i.e.*, protected game. Absurd as it was, this legal anomaly seemed to be understood by the beasts themselves, which kept to the Matabeleland side and avoided the opposite one.

On the Pungwe flats, during the railway construction from Fontesvilla to Mashonaland and for some time after the line was opened, immense herds of buffalo, numbering several thousands of head, and mixed troops of *wilde-beeste* (brindled gnu) and zebra, nearly as large, were often seen by passengers travelling on the train ; but that was before the outbreak of rinderpest, which wrought deadly havoc among ruminant animals, wild as well as domestic.

From what survived in these two neighbouring territories one could form an idea of the magnificent spectacle which the veld of Mashonaland must have presented to the hunters of the nineteenth century almost up to the arrival of the Pioneers, and it seems hard that the disappearance of grand creatures like the giraffe and the total extinction of such species as the white rhinoceros should be the inevitable sequel of European settlement. Two of the latter were shot in 1893, near Lomagunda by Mr. (afterwards Sir Robert) Coryndon, and were the last seen in Mashonaland, where they were, within the memory of living men, among the commonest, and certainly the least ferocious of the great pachyderms. Mr. Coryndon's pair were carefully mounted and sent, one to Lord Rothschild's private collection, and the other to the Capetown Museum, where it can still be seen.

The trivial hunting experiences which fell to the lot of most of us in those early years are not worth telling. Those who want the real thing can find it in the delightful narratives published by the late F. C. Selous. Incidentally he was the most modest of men where his own exploits were concerned and could seldom be drawn into talking about them. It is curious, however, that when a story of sport is told there is always some one who tries to cap it. A certain Major Hamilton

Browne—commonly known as " Maori " Brown, on the strength of his picturesque tales of real or imaginary adventures in New Zealand—was a man of this sort, albeit a most amusing *raconteur* of the Munchausen type. At the police officers' mess in Salisbury the conversation turned one evening on snakes, and somebody asked Selous, who was present, whether he had known any interesting cases of pythons swallowing their prey whole. Selous replied that he had once killed a python which had gorged itself with an ant-bear whose body was found half-digested in its interior. This gave an opening to Maori Browne, who promptly recounted a circumstantial yarn of a victorious personal encounter in Natal with an enormous python which, on being cut open, revealed the complete carcase of a trek ox ! Everybody gasped, and Selous quietly asked " What about the horns ? " Maori had overlooked this detail, but realised that his reputation was at stake and that he must see the matter through. Only pausing to take a gulp at his whiskey and soda he boldly, and without visible embarrassment, took up the challenge. " Horns and all, my dear boy," he replied. " Horns and all ! "

Elephants, which were fairly plentiful throughout Mashonaland in Selous' time, betook themselves after the occupation to the remoter districts. Occasionally a few would find their way to some of the outlying farms and do much damage to standing crops. About 1908, a herd became such a nuisance to farmers in the Lomagundi district that the Government temporarily suspended the clause in the regulations which protected them as " Royal " game, and several residents of Salisbury, anxious to seize this opportunity of a rare sport, made up expeditions with a view to trying their luck during the week end. But, while they were arranging their plans, a party of Boers stole a march on them, trekked out to Lomagundi on horse-back, followed by their waggons, and within a few days had slaughtered the whole herd, numbering, I think, about 30. They traded some of the meat to the natives and made the remainder into biltong, which, together with a large number of sjamboks cut from the hides, they brought into Salisbury for sale.

About the same time the mail train, on its way from the Victoria Falls to Bulawayo, collided by night with a large bull elephant which was strolling along the railway line. A certain amount of injury was done to the engine, but the train was, fortunately, not derailed. As generally happens to pedestrians, the elephant came off worst and was, of course, put out of his suffering by a bullet. The railway company appropriated the ivory, which they realised to such advantage that they were able to defray the cost of repairing the damage to their engine.

Travellers, especially when using pack-donkeys to carry their kit and provisions, were often bothered by lions. One of the pioneers—Clay by name—having to make a camp by night in a district infested by these beasts, enclosed his donkeys within a stout *scherm* of thorn-bushes, and at one side of it pitched his patrol tent, where he retired to rest with his clothes and boots on and a loaded rifle by his side. In the middle of the night he was roused by a tremendous snorting and grunting and springing up found his donkeys plunging about in the darkness and straining at their head ropes. One of them had apparently broken loose and seemed to Clay, who could only dimly discern its outline, to be trying to leap over the fence. So he walked up and in order to turn it back gave it a couple of hard kicks in the ribs. The response to this was an angry growl. " A donkey that growls," thought he, " must be a *lusus naturae*, and is better out of the way." So he laid it low with a bullet at about two yards range, and, lighting a lantern, found that what he had been kicking was a fine male lion. The late Mr. Alexander Boggie, a prominent trader at Lobengula's kraal, was less fortunate, for, hearing a disturbance in his camp one night and suspecting lions, he poured a charge of " loopers " at close quarters into a shadowy figure which, he thought, was charging him and found a minute afterwards that he had bagged one of his own donkeys. He endured the resultant banter with stoicism, and never turned a hair when someone asked him if he would send the skin to Messrs. Rowland Ward for mounting. Some years later he wrote a pleasant little book of his experiences in Matabeleland but omitted to record this episode.

One characteristic of lions—and other beasts of prey as well— was their unexpectedness. You might go hunting for days in known lion-veld without finding even the spoor of one ; on the other hand, you might be out for a quiet ride near your home without a rifle and run into a family party. Long after Salisbury had grown into an established town, with shops and brick buildings, a lioness strolled down Pioneer Street one Sunday afternoon, when most of the inhabitants were having a nap. She snapped up an unsuspecting bull-terrier—the only living thing she could see—which was dozing on the stoep of the Masonic hotel, and retired with her kill into the long grass at the back of the kopje, where she was routed out and despatched the same evening.

It was just the same with crocodiles. They had a discourteous habit of turning up unannounced. Dr. Rutherfoord Harris, the Secretary of the Chartered Company, went for a swim one afternoon in the Hanyani River, not far from Salisbury —rather a foolhardy thing to do—and afterwards sat, still in his birthday suit, on a rock at the edge of the stream and trimmed his toe-nails. While he was engaged in this absorbing task a crocodile crept stealthily up and attacked him from behind, inflicting severe wounds, which kept him in hospital for some weeks, and eventually necessitated his leaving the country.

This was a most unusual occurrence in Mashonaland, for although crocodiles were plentiful in all the rivers, they were seldom bold enough to attack human beings. But they were very destructive to goats, young cattle, and even donkeys, seizing them by the head while drinking and holding them under water till drowned. Constant warfare was waged against them by white men. The usual weapon employed was dynamite or a detonator cartridge with a lighted fuse affixed to it. This was thrown into one of the detached pools of which in the dry season many of the streams are composed. The shock of the explosion stunned the crocodile (if there happened to be one), and caused it to rise to the surface, where it was easily despatched. White miners and prospectors accustomed to explosives also used this method for catching fish, and were very reckless in handling the detonators, sometimes even biting them to make them clip the fuse. In this way a ghastly accident befel one of the pioneers, Edward Suckling. The detonator exploded in his face, half of which it blew away, besides blinding him, so that his death, which followed a day or two later, was a merciful release.

This carelessness in handling explosives extended to firearms, even with men thoroughly used to them, as most of us were. My old friend Mr. Cooper Chadwick, a good sportsman and a fine shot, was standing with his hands resting on the muzzle of his loaded gun, when his little dog, which was fawning on him, caught the trigger with its fore-paw. The gun went off, and the charge passed through both hands, necessitating a double amputation. That was thirty-six years ago, and Mr. Chadwick, in spite of his severe handicap, has taught himself to do with his stumps nearly as much as other men can with their fingers. His handwriting is particularly clear, and he has published an interesting book—the manuscript of which I have seen—of his experiences during a three years' residence at Lobengula's kraal.

To return to our crocodiles. On the Zambesi River they are much bolder where human beings are concerned, and some think

Black Rhinoceros

A Maneater

this is due to their having acquired the man-eating habit in days past, when powerful native chiefs punished offenders and rid themselves of enemies by binding their hands and feet and throwing them into the river. I have heard of cases where a crocodile has knocked a native paddler out of a canoe by a swish from its powerful tail, but cannot vouch for this as a fact. The villagers on the banks of the river, and especially the women, are to this day very stupid about exposing themselves to attack. In 1903 I was at Kazangula, an old ferrying-point on the Zambesi, when one of a party of women who were washing clothes in the river near the bank, and standing up to their knees in the water, was seized and carried off by a man-eating crocodile. Her companions fled screaming, and all that day there was loud lamentation in the village, and no one ventured near the river, but on the following morning they were all back again, wading about and laughing and chatting, quite unconcerned at the danger. Small wonder that women's bangles and other metal ornaments are from time to time found in the paunches of crocodiles shot on the Zambesi River.

However, in Mashonaland "crocks" were not such a common danger as to cause us any sleepless nights. I wish I could say the same about some of the smaller vermin which followed us into our homes. Rats, for instance, during the first two or three years, were an intolerable plague. Besides eating our provisions, candles and boots, they would attack people when asleep, nibble their hair and gnaw the tips of their fingers. By day they used to play hide and seek behind the native-made cane mats with which we lined the sides and ceilings of our huts. We could hear them chirruping to one another, and follow their movements by the agitation of the mats as they scampered up and down. They were fond of carrying anything portable to their nests, and we once discovered a whole linen table-cloth tucked away in a rat hole—greatly to the relief of the houseboy who had been accused of the theft.

Then there were the insect pests which buzzed about in clouds whenever a lamp or candle was lit—beetles, large and small, flopping in the soup and crawling down our necks ; mosquitoes ; midges—sometimes in such dense swarms that we had to swathe our heads in towels in order to have a meal in peace ; an occasional scorpion, and creeping things innumerable. Never, I suppose, was there such a rich field for the study of entomology, and yet, with one exception, we were blind to our opportunities, and, instead of devoting ourselves to scientific research, we only indulged in bad language. The exception was Mr. G. A. K. Marshall, now I believe professor of entomology, and one of the greatest authorities on " bugs " in the world. At that time Mr. Marshall was a civil servant in Salisbury, and he alone, being a true philosopher, saw that what merely provoked the many could be turned to profit for himself.

I must not forget the ubiquitous termites, or " white ants," as everyone calls them, so plentiful and voracious in places that the feet of tables and cupboards had to be stood in saucers of paraffin to keep these little pests from tunnelling up the legs. As for clothes and books, unless one inspected them constantly or kept them in airtight steel boxes, the ants would in a few hours consume every part of them except the bare outside.

That the life history of the termite is as yet imperfectly understood will be gathered from the following incident, for the truth of which others besides myself can vouch.

Two or three professional men who took their meals at one of the most " fashionable " hotels in Bulawayo had reason to suspect that the whiskey supplied to them was being regularly watered. They sent for the manager, who was profuse in his protestations that nothing of the sort could possibly happen in his establishment, and, as a proof of his *bona fides*, offered to open a new bottle in their presence. The bottle was brought —a well-known and favourite brand—and the manager pointed out that the lead capsule was unbroken and the cork intact. He then personally opened the bottle and poured a tot into one of the glasses, but was rather taken aback when, with the whiskey, out came an unmistakable white ant !

I began this chapter with some remarks on lions, and before closing would say that during a long residence in Rhodesia I never had a shot at a lion nor went out of my way to meet them, though I did so on several occasions when I was unarmed. My attitude towards lions has always been that of the late Mr. " Ikey " Sonnenburg, a celebrated trader who frequented Rhodesia in the early nineties. He was at Victoria, and lions had been doing damage to stock at some farms close to the commonage, so a party of two or three sportsmen started very early one Sunday morning to try and round them up. As they walked down the street with their dogs and rifles they passed Ikey, who, clad in his pyjamas, was sniffing the morning air at the door of his store. " Where are you boys off to ? " he enquired. " We're going to look for the lions," they replied. " Will you come along with us ? " " No, thank ye," said Ikey," I ain't lost no lions."

CHAPTER XII.

" Loben."

Most of the human obstacles encountered by Rhodes in reconstructing the map of Africa were either out-manœuvred or " absorbed." There were two, however, with whom neither of these methods succeeded—President Krüger and " King " Lobengula—and of them the latter is, I think, the more deserving of sympathy and admiration.

" Oom Paul's " sole interest in the Englishmen who swarmed into his country after the discovery of gold was as a means of aggrandisement for his own people and enrichment of his treasury. He tolerated them only in so far as they submitted to be bled without aspiring to political freedom. Although he proved too hard a nut for Rhodes to crack, he utterly misjudged the British temperament, and thereby compassed his own destruction.

" Loben," on the other hand, was the victim of inexorable circumstances. Equally with Krüger, he was anxious to protect the traditions and liberties of his own people, but very early in the day he realised that the English would not be denied. He made an honest endeavour to prevent a clash between two irreconcilable forces, and when the fates proved too strong for him he made his exit like a gentleman.

The Matabele régime was a survival from the time when African tribes lived by preying on one another ; when outrage and robbery were the roads to prosperity, and when Chiefs maintained their authority only by a callous disregard of human life. Loben's father, the founder of the Matabele nation, was aptly named Mziligazi—" the trail of blood." His young braves were trained to look upon other tribes as existing merely to provide them with profit and amusement. Fighting was their profession and murder their pastime. They depended on their raids for cattle to augment their own herds, for youths to incorporate into their own regiments, and for girls to become their slave wives. Any adult man or old woman so unfortunate as to fall into their hands they butchered with every refinement of brutal and sadistic torture. With the possible exceptions of the Masai of Uganda and the Touaregs of the French Sahara,

89

they were the fiercest and most relentless of all the savage races inhabiting Africa.

Twenty years before the occupation of Mashonaland, Lobengula had succeeded to the sovereignty of this pack of human wolves, and had thereby become pledged to perpetuate the methods by which they terrorised the other tribes between the Zambesi and Crocodile Rivers. He could never have maintained his authority or the iron discipline needful to keep alive the spirit of his warriors had he not been a man of unusual force of character ; but he also had the advantage of a powerful instrument in the shape of a hierarchy of wizards. The belief in witchcraft pervaded the whole life and social economy of the tribe to a degree which it is difficult for European minds to grasp. The weather, the failure or success of the harvest, the result of expeditions against other tribes, even the petty fortunes and misfortunes of family life, were, in the eyes of the Matabele, governed by supernatural agencies whose favour could be legitimately invoked only by the official magic-mongers. They were a close corporation, and, like the British Medical Council, exacted the direst penalties from unregistered practitioners. The Matabele, in common with most Bantu natives, regarded deaths or diseases, whether of men or cattle, not as due to natural causes, but as the result of illicit sorcery, and when any such event occurred looked to the wizards to discover and punish the authors. The power thus enjoyed by these officials was utilised by the King for the purpose of getting rid of any subject who grew too prosperous or in other ways excited his suspicion. All such were denounced as illegally dabbling in magic, and were condemned to death—sometimes with their families—by being knocked on the head or thrown to the crocodiles. The King himself was the central figure of the system, and was Grand Master of the ceremonies by which the destiny of the nation, alike with the fate of individuals, was influenced. To what extent he was himself deluded it is difficult to say, but he took his part in the mystic hocus-pocus which custom demanded with great punctilio, especially when presiding at the annual rites connected with rain-making, the waging of war and the detection of individuals suspected of hatching treason.

Judged by native standards, Loben was a sound constitutional monarch, and one who kept the interests of his people constantly in the forefront. He cannot be blamed for his fidelity to the traditions which he had inherited from his Zulu ancestors, but the remarkable thing is that, steeped as he was in these traditions, he had the sense to appreciate the civilized

The Indaba Tree

point of view, and to make a real effort to modify his own system so as to ward off the doom which he alone of all his people saw threatening it. That peace was maintained between his hot-headed young soldiers and the Englishmen who entered his country—not only during the years preceding the occupation of Mashonaland, when the stream of immigration was a thin trickle, but for three years afterwards, when it was in full flood—was due mainly to Loben's diplomacy. From the very start the dice were loaded against him ; but he played the game with skill and dignity, and never cheated.

I never saw Lobengula myself, and of the white men who visited Bulawayo in his time very few—possibly not half-a-dozen—survive. Col. Frank Johnson, Mr. Ben Wilson (" Matabele Wilson "), Mr. E. A. Maund, Mr. Cooper Chadwick and Mr. W. E. Thomas are the only ones I can think of. From all of these, and from others no longer alive, I have heard that he was a native of majestic build and dignified personality. He usually wore nothing but a roll of dark blue cloth and a sporran or apron of monkey-skin ; but on ceremonial occasions, such as the great annual dance held in February, he donned full war paint, with bands of otter-skin and long crane-feathers. On his scalp was the usual Zulu head-ring worn by all married men, and when he walked he carried a long staff in his hand. A French explorer, M. Lionel Décle, who visited him in 1891, wrote : " I have seen many European and native potentates, and, with the exception of the Tsar Alexander, never have I seen a ruler of men with a more imposing appearance." Although he had a brick house in Bulawayo, he preferred to sleep in a Cape ox-waggon, and in this travelled to his other favourite kraals. His chair of state was under the " indaba tree," a large wild plum with gnarled roots which is still preserved in the garden of the house built by Rhodes on the site of Loben's residence. Here he used to grant interviews, dispense justice and settle tribal disputes, while his courtiers crouched in front of him, punctuating his utterances with extravagant compliments. White men attending these palavers were expected to partake of the beef and Kaffir beer which were provided in large quantities for the consumption of the King and his court, being brought in by female attendants, who had to sip from each pot of liquor before it was handed to the Chief.

To such an extent was Loben successful in keeping the peace that by 1893 we, in Mashonaland, had almost forgotten the Matabele who for fifty years had been the bogey of South Africa. They had never molested us—had apparently ceased to bother about us. Old stagers who preached caution, and recalled the many native risings in Natal and Cape Colony, found that they were derided as funks or alarmists, and so they held their tongues. The rest of us went about our affairs in happy indifference to the volcano on whose edge we lived.

Consequently we were rather incredulous when a telegram reached Salisbury one morning in July, 1893, with the news that a Matabele raid of the real, old-fashioned sort was actually in progress round Victoria, the new mining township, which was nearest to Lobengula's outlying kraals and cattle-posts. There was, however, no mistake about it. A couple of regiments sent by him to punish one of his petty chiefs for theft had got out of hand, crossed the border and begun attacking and burning Mashona villages, spearing the unfortunate occupants and driving off their cattle. Some of the Mashonas fled towards Victoria, whither they were pursued by the raiders, who killed many of them within sight of the astonished settlers, and demanded the surrender of those who had gained sanctuary in the township itself. Included among their victims was a mission boy employed by the English chaplain. This last was a grave error of judgment on the part of the raiders, and was made the most of by those who cried out for retaliation. The townspeople kept their heads, and for the time being contented themselves with putting the fort in a state of defence and holding themselves ready to take the field, while they awaited the coming of the "Doctor," who hurried down from Salisbury to tackle the unexpected crisis. On arrival he sent for the leaders of the Matabele and gave them two hours in which to clear over the border. To enforce his order, he despatched a party of mounted volunteers, who, finding that some of the raiders were still burning and looting in the neighbourhood of the town commonage, opened fire and inflicted heavy punishment on them.

This was the " Victoria incident," for which the Chartered Company and the brutal settlers were pilloried by the Aborigines Protection Society and other busy-bodies of the Exeter Hall school, whose faces were aglow with what Rhodes called "unctuous rectitude," and who were unable to believe that their own countrymen could by any possibility have a righteous cause.

This is not the place to tell the story of the Matabele war. It was short and, as far as it went, decisive. The brunt of the fighting was borne by the 700 citizen-soldiers from Salisbury and Victoria, who, led by Jameson in person, advanced upon Matabeleland and, after routing several of Loben's crack regiments in a couple of sharp engagements, marched into his capital,

Bulawayo, the "Place of Slaughter." They found that the Chief himself, with the rest of his fighting men, had taken flight after firing the great kraal and blowing up the stores of ammunition which it contained.

The only human beings left in the smoking ruins were two English traders, who had remained in Bulawayo throughout the fighting, confident that Loben would not allow them to be killed or even molested, and in spite of the pressure that had been brought to bear upon him, the old savage had not betrayed them.

By the majority of the settlers the blow which Jameson's audacious coup had inflicted on the Matabele was regarded as a "knock-out," but two causes helped to make the conquest incomplete. The first was the advent of the rainy season, which brought down the rivers and stopped all movement of troops. The one patrol that was sent in pursuit of Loben was compelled to return seriously crippled by the loss of Alan Wilson and his 33 brave companions, who, when the fugitive appeared to be within their grasp, were surrounded and cut down to a man. This should have proved that the Matabele army still had a sting in its tail. The other cause was the interference of the Home Government, who were urged by short-sighted humanitarians to prevent Jameson from effecting a complete disarmament of the natives. Lord Ripon stupidly yielded to pressure and ordered him to stay his hand. The natives construed this as a sign of weakness. They hid away their rifles and assegais and cunningly waited for another opportunity to use them.

But the days of the unhappy Lobengula, who had striven so hard to fend off disaster, were numbered. He had made a last belated effort to stop the war by tendering an indemnity of £1,000, but this was foiled by the dishonesty of a couple of troopers, into whose hands the bag of sovereigns accidentally fell. Not long afterwards the pursuit of the Chief was abandoned and an attempt made to open negotiations for his surrender, but before Jameson's emissaries could reach him he was stricken down, some say by smallpox, but more probably by despair aggravated by exposure to the weather and the vicissitudes of his flight.

Even before Bulawayo was occupied rumours had been current that Lobengula possessed a vast treasure in gold coin, uncut diamonds and elephant tusks, and immediately after the entry of the troops the blackened debris of his quarters and storehouses was carefully raked over in the hope of recovering booty. As far as I can remember, the only article of value brought to light was the model of an elephant in silver, said to have been presented to him by the Directors of the Tati Concessions. The remains of several sporting rifles were also discovered but nothing which could be called " treasure." When the Chief fled he was known to have had with him only four waggons, and while it would have been easy for him to have taken away diamonds and specie he could not have carried off any large quantity of tusks. It was hastily assumed, therefore, that his collection of ivory had been destroyed by the fire, though had this been the case the charred remains would certainly have been found.

Not long afterwards, stories were circulated that before his flight the Chief had made arrangements for depositing his treasure in a safe hiding-place known only to himself and two or three trusted subjects, and to this day there are people who are convinced that the hoard still exists. A half-breed, Jacobs, who had acted as letter-writer to Loben during the war and accompanied him on his flight traded for many years on a real or pretended knowledge of the *cache*, and offered to reveal it for a money reward. Several times he succeeded in obtaining advances from white men, but, as he had over a dozen convictions for cattle theft and other crimes recorded against him, he was always intercepted by the police and deported, before his knowledge could be put to the test.

There can be no doubt whatever that Loben had, for many years before his downfall, been accumulating treasure. All savage despots in the interior of Africa possessed hoards of ivory varying in amount according to the number of subordinate tribes over which they held sway. Ivory in the tusk was the recognised form in which tribute was exacted from conquered enemies. It was also the symbol of submission, and both before and after the rebellion in Rhodesia tusks were voluntarily given to the Chartered Company by petty chiefs as a token of their loyalty and desire for peace. Apart from what he may have collected himself, Lobengula must have inherited a great quantity from his father Mziligazi, the biggest marauder of all, who carried on raiding expeditions for thirty years before his death in 1868. Hoards of ivory were usually buried underground ; but, even if Loben had kept his collection in store-huts, it is impossible that it should have been so utterly consumed by the fire which destroyed his kraal as to have left no trace. There is every justification therefore for the belief that somewhere in the neighbourhood of Bulawayo a great quantity of buried tusks lies waiting to be unearthed.

Then, as regards diamonds, I have been told by natives and old traders that, in the 'seventies and 'eighties, Loben used to stipulate that every Matabele working at the Kimberley diggings should give him one stone on his return, and, as large numbers of them used to go to the diamond fields, he may have amassed a substantial hoard in this way. If it had been dispersed at the time of his flight or after his death, some of the stones would inevitably have come to light, but nothing of this sort happened except once, in 1894, when John Jacobs, who had surrendered to the authorities, was sent to Salisbury to be detained as a " political prisoner." As Magistrate, I saw him the day after his arrival, when Mr. Swemmer, the gaoler, reported that, on searching him, he found that he was in possession of three or four small uncut diamonds, and that, on being questioned, he stated that he knew where a large store of stones, " filling two paraffin tins," was hidden. When I interviewed Jacobs, he had the audacity to offer to lead me to the spot if I would procure his release ! Some time later he was discharged—not, however, through my agency—and deported. There is nothing inherently impossible in the existence of the hoard, though the paraffin tins were probably an artistic invention of Jacobs.

As for gold coin, it is unlikely that Loben had much hoarded, for, although the Chartered Company had paid him £100 in sovereigns every month from October, 1888, to July, 1893—i.e., between £5,000 and £6,000—there were always heavy demands on his privy purse. Some of his wives, of whom there were forty or fifty, and especially his head consort Losikeyi, a lady whose greed was only equalled by her embonpoint, acquired a taste for champagne and for other European goods such as beads, fancy blankets and coloured calico, and were regular customers at the stores kept by the white traders at Bulawayo. Still, he must have had a fair sum of money with him when he took to flight, witness that bag of gold which he sent to Jameson as a peace offering. It is significant also that at a later date a visit to Bulawayo by his corpulent widow Losikeyi coincided with the sudden appearance there of a considerable number of pre-Victorian gold coins of an issue which had long been withdrawn from circulation.

All these little bits of evidence, taken together, lead to the irresistible conclusion that a large treasure did exist, and that it was not dispersed. If that is admitted, it follows that it is still concealed somewhere in Matabeleland and that there may be a fine haul one of these days for some lucky fossicker. It is as likely as not that the hiding-place is near the site of the Chief's favourite kraal, which was not Bulawayo, but Emvutjwa, a few miles to the north.

CHAPTER XIII.

A Boom and a Slump.

Few episodes of Colonial history have more profoundly stirred popular sentiment than the tragic catastrophe of the Shangani River, where a handful of the Mashonaland Volunteers —not trained soldiers, but just miners, farmers, clerks and traders—fired with the desire for achievement, fell into a trap and died, shoulder to shoulder, in a splendid but hopeless dash to capture the Matabele King. No doubt the emotion caused by their exploit was partly inspired by the uncertainty that for a long while hung over the actual details, some of which will never be known—for there was no survivor.

Allan Wilson, their leader, was a cool-headed Highlander, a man of well-knit, powerful frame, who had spent some years as a frontier policeman, and had become manager of one of the mining syndicates working in Victoria. Those who went out with him on that last fateful ride, cheerily calling out to their messmates, as they cantered off, to keep supper hot for them, were all in the heyday of manhood, many of them trained in the public schools and universities of England and Scotland, and the rest tough Colonials well used to campaigning in Africa. They were the very flower of the settlers, and, although there was no special selection of individuals to form the patrol, it would have been difficult to have picked a couple of score men better fitted to give a good account of themselves in a tight place. Indeed, it was some time before the rest of us in Salisbury and Bulawayo could bring ourselves to believe that so brave a company had been wiped out to a man by the broken and fugitive remnants of Lobengula's army. Native reports said that the King was still shaping his course for Mashonaland with Wilson's party hard on his heels. To this idea we clung, and it was some weeks before we grasped the full force of the disaster which had overtaken the patrol actually on its very first day.

During that last month of 1893 there was a good deal of unrest among the Mashona tribes bordering on Matabeleland. A party of three or four prospectors was attacked at a village 90 or 100 miles to the north-west of Salisbury, and one of them— Arthur Stanford by name—fatally wounded. On Christmas

Some Officers of Victoria Column, 1893

Standing (left to right) : Lieut. Stoddart, Captain Judd, Major Allan Wilson, Captain Napier, Captain Fitzgerald, Lieut. Hamilton, Lieut. Williams. *Seated* : Lieut. Sampson, Adjutant Kennedy.

Eve I was sent out to hold a magisterial inquiry into this affair, and, on account of the excited state of the natives, an escort of twenty-five police with a maxim gun under the command of Inspector Randolph Nesbitt (who afterwards gained the V.C.) was detailed to accompany me, but the rainy season was at its height, and their progress was much delayed by flooded rivers. I, therefore, pushed ahead with an interpreter and had completed my inquiry before they caught me up. We had started on the return journey when we were met by a mounted trooper from Salisbury, who brought information that Loben was reported to be making for the Lomagunda district with Wilson's patrol in hot pursuit, and handed orders to Nesbitt and myself to endeavour to get into touch with the latter and give them assistance. We, therefore, turned back, with ten of the best-mounted men, and spent several days in visiting kraal after kraal and following clues that invariably proved false. The natives were manifestly in a state of nervous excitement, and probably thought that the presence of our patrol would bring the Matabele down upon them. To get rid of us they concocted a story that Loben, pursued by a party of white men, had followed the Angwa River towards Portuguese territory, and accordingly we bent our steps in the same direction. In a few days we found ourselves in a belt of tsetse fly, with no food for our horses or rations for ourselves, and in country so waterlogged by the torrential rains as to make further progress impossible. I sent a couple of Cape boys forward with such food as was available and with letters for the Portuguese Governor of Zumbo, but afterwards learnt that both of them died of fever. We made a difficult journey back, having to swim several swollen rivers, and on arrival in Salisbury found that the authorities had received intelligence which left no doubt of the fate of Wilson and his comrades, though it was some weeks before the death of Loben was definitely established.

During this patrol I visited for the first time the strange limestone caverns of Sinoia, with their mysterious subterranean lake of unfathomable depth, whose brilliant ultramarine hue is equalled only by that of the celebrated grotto of Capri. The railway has long since made Sinoia a favourite week-end resort for Salisbury townspeople, but at that time very few white men had seen the caves.

After the stampede of Loben and his army, Mashonaland settled down to a period of utter stagnation, for all interest was concentrated on the new province. The bulk of our fellow-settlers had gone with Jameson to the front, and, as they were rewarded with farms and gold-claims, they had every temptation to remain in Matabeleland. Pioneers, and especially those in quest of gold, are easily attracted to fresh fields, and the excitement of winning a new country was intensified by thrilling reports of reefs far exceeding in richness anything which had been found in Mashonaland. An influx of new Colonists set in from the South, and even from England, and in the rush which ensued very few troubled to make the additional journey of 300 miles to reach Salisbury, while the number of those arriving from the East through Beira was almost negligible. As for Victoria the eclipse there was total. For two years before the war it had been the main centre of mining activity and actually boasted of a producing mine—the "Dickens," where a five-stamp battery had been erected and a small output of gold declared. It had also been the half-way house on the Pioneer road to Salisbury and the meeting place of the weekly mail-carts from the North and South. Passengers in both directions generally spent a night or two there, and the "Thatched House" hotel did a thriving trade. Now all traffic was diverted to the more direct route along the watershed to Matabeleland, and poor Victoria was left completely in the cold. The little township relapsed into an oblivion which lasted for twenty years, and was nearly as complete as that which for centuries enveloped the neighbouring ruins of Zimbabwe.

Those of us who stuck to Salisbury also felt the draught severely. The splendid advertisement which Bulawayo had received through the sensational events of the occupation was taken full advantage of by the Chartered Company. What they wanted was capital to develop the resources of the country, and capital now began to flow in like water. Everything was done to keep the movement alive. A city was planned on most ambitious lines near the site of Lobengula's kraal. Jameson said he would have streets wide enough for a bullock-waggon to turn in. He got them, and thereby laid up a heavy burden for future Town Councils which have still to keep them in order though the bullock waggons are no longer there. A sale of building plots was held and fabulous prices were realised. Rapidly a great straggling township of corrugated iron spread over the plain where, but a year or two before, the *impis* of the Matabele had paraded for their annual war-dances in all the glory of ostrich feather plumes and long ox-hide shields. Waterworks were started ; electric light installed ; hotels with high-sounding names—the "Palace," the "Maxim," the "Imperial" —clubs, churches, and stores sprang up like magic. There was

Salisbury in 1896

Ruins of Lobengula's House, Bulawayo, 1893

even a Stock Exchange, and a " Silver Grill," where quite nice lunches were obtainable at about £1 a head. Rhodes took a hand and built himself a roomy bungalow in the Cape Dutch style on the very site of Loben's house, now a crumbling mass of gutted ruins. He also pushed forward the construction of the railway from the South so as to shorten the immense distance over which every commodity of life had still to be dragged by oxen.

In Salisbury we heard of these things and envied. We did not even get the overflow of all this prosperity. We still had our dismal black swamp in the middle of the town, and our ramshackle " Kyas " of wattle and daub. By 1894, it is true, there was a sprinkling of brick stores and offices and a few wells had been sunk, but the majority of us lived in thatched huts and had to get our drinking water up from the river below the camp in barrels hauled by donkeys or perspiring natives.

There was no electric light for us. Those who were bold enough to venture out after dark had to carry a lantern to save them from falling into dagga-pits or the open ditches which drained the camp. Social intercourse was in consequence mainly restricted to the daytime or to bright moonlight nights. There is a story of two bachelor friends at Salisbury who had formed a practice of dining alternately at each other's huts on Saturday evenings. Once they sat late into the night, discussing no doubt some political question, and parted company only when the supply of " square-face " ran short. Early next morning he who had been the host was roused by the arrival of his friend's boy with the following note :—

" Dear Jim,
    " I think I left my hurricane lamp at your hut last night. Please send it back by the bearer.
                                    " Yours, GEORGE.
" P.S.—I am returning the cage containing your parrot."

Nominally Salisbury still remained the administrative capital of the country, but in reality it was an isolated up-country " dorp " where a few bored Civil servants struggled to kill time and a few traders made a precarious living by ministering to their requirements.

Our amusements in those dull days were limited to indifferent golf and cricket and to an occasional shooting expedition into the surrounding veld. We were, of course, better off than the lonely farmers and Government officials in the outside districts, who, apart from shooting, had no amusements at all. The farmers had their herds and crops to attend to ; but the officials made pathetic efforts to fill in their leisure. One Native Commissioner spent months in laying out a nine-hole golf course at his station. When at length it was completed, he used to play a round every evening by himself, and for this purpose always donned the scarlet jacket which was demanded by fashion in those days. Golf was by no means so universal a game as it is to-day, but most settlements of any pretension had their links. At one little township—not Salisbury—the golf-course lay just beyond the cemetery, and I happened to be there one day when a funeral was taking place. Most of the inhabitants were friends of the deceased and followed his remains to the graveside, and, in the procession of mourners marching in couples behind the bier, I noticed that two were carrying their golf-clubs.

Salisbury was naturally a very healthy camp, with a cool and pleasant climate, but in the wet season pools of water were allowed to collect and become the breeding places of mosquitoes, with the result that malaria was very prevalent. A mild dose was not regarded by us as an unmixed evil, for it meant a pleasant spell of comfort in the little hospital under the gentle ministrations of Mother Patrick and her staff of Dominican nursing nuns. In fact, I regret to say that various ruses were practised to prolong the treatment and were encouraged by the guileless innocence of these devoted ladies. It was their custom, for instance, to take the temperatures of the patients at tea-time, and what was more easy, when the nurse's back was turned, than to dip the thermometer for a few seconds in the hot tea by the bedside and, when the mercury rose to 101 deg. or 102 deg., to replace it in one's mouth ?

Towards the close of the wet season the malaria assumed a more virulent form, and a good many cases of blackwater fever were brought into Salisbury from the mining districts—often too late for medical treatment to be of any avail. In the first year after the occupation those who died had generally to be buried in their blankets, for it was impossible to obtain the wherewithal to make coffins. About this time a popular pioneer fell a victim to fever and his friends went to great trouble to put together a shell made of ordinary packing-case wood, which for appearance sake they concealed beneath a Union Jack. When, however, the rough-and-ready coffin was uncovered at the graveside, the spectators were rather startled to see revealed in stencilled letters on the top the words, " Stow in a Cool Place."

This reminds me that in another of the early townships all funeral arrangements were carried out by a serious-minded Scotsman whose only frivolous characteristic was a taste for the bagpipes. He was a fairly skilful performer and was consequently in request at Caledonian gatherings. On St. Andrew's Day he always attended the evening banquet in Highland costume and " piped in " the haggis, marching in front of it with grave and measured step. The grisly suggestiveness of the undertaker's share in this ceremony was not lost upon any Englishmen present, but it never seemed to impair the appetites of the assembled Scotsmen.

The boom in Bulawayo and the corresponding depression in Salisbury lasted till the close of 1895, and, although there were rumblings and threats of trouble in Johannesburg, they were too distant to excite any particular anxiety in Rhodesia, and certainly failed to warn us of the explosion which was to shake our very foundations in the last few days of the year. Some of us were rather curious as to the energy which the " Doctor " displayed in the organisation of the Rhodesia Horse, a new regiment of volunteers, with divisions at Salisbury and Bulawayo, and wondered whether some new adventure might be in the air. The removal, however, at the end of October of several hundred of our own police to the neighbourhood of Mafeking, near the Transvaal border, aroused very little interest, at any rate, in Salisbury, for we had heard that the Chartered Company was to take over the administration of a large portion of the Protectorate, and the transfer of police seemed a natural precaution against possible disturbance among the Bechuana tribes, who had already shown uneasiness at the advance of the railway. Nobody knew anything definite, though there were a few who spoke confidently of a projected expedition to annex the unknown territories north of the Zambesi. On the strength of this rumour, most of us joined the Volunteers, and, having pleasant memories of the occupation, first of Mashonaland and then of Matabeleland, we ate our Christmas dinners with good appetites and a cheerful anticipation of livelier times to come in 1896.

Well, well ! We hadn't long to wait !

CHAPTER XIV.

REBELLION.

ON the 3rd of January, 1896, a jolly company of eleven men and two women foregathered at a private house in Greenwood, on the outskirts of Salisbury, to celebrate the New Year. Another expected guest wrote at the last moment to excuse herself on the ground of a slight dose of fever, and so, with a little chaff but no serious forebodings, we sat down to dinner thirteen. It was an ill-omened beginning of a year of tragedy. Before it closed several of the men present lost the number of their mess, and within six months both the women perished in the wreck of the " Drummond Castle " off Ushant.

One of the party was Mr. Joseph Vintcent, then acting as head of the Government in the absence of the "`Doctor,`" of whose whereabouts we were uncertain, though he was thought to be in the Bechuanaland Protectorate arranging with the Imperial authorities for its transfer to the Chartered Company. Owing to some interruption in the telegraph service—quite a common occurrence in those times—we had for several days been cut off from communication with the outer world—not that this damped our spirits, for at Salisbury we were a little world of our own with plenty of domestic and social concerns to keep us amused. Still when, half-way through dinner, a fat brown envelope from the Telegraph Office was brought in by a messenger and handed to Vintcent, who announced that it contained belated " Reuters," and asked permission to read them, the general conversation was politely hushed, and with mild interest we prepared to hear the list of New Year's honours, the usual items about Armenian atrocities, the market fluctuations in wheat and cotton and so forth.

Our calm detachment was shattered by the first electric words :—

Capetown, 31st December.—Great excitement caused here by news that Dr. Jameson has crossed Transvaal border with 800 mounted men with maxim and field guns. High Commissioner and Chartered Company repudiate his action, and former has sent two telegrams demanding his instant return   .   .   ."

Thrill followed thrill as Vintcent, in tones now exultant, now husky with grief, read out the first Press version of the " Raid "—the letter from the Reform Committee at Johannesburg begging Jameson to come to the relief of " unarmed men, women and children at the mercy of well-armed Boers " ; the impetuous start of the Police from Pitsani ; their forced march through the Transvaal ; their hopeless battle against superior odds at Krugersdorp, and then the final paralysing account of their surrender at Doornkop. Good heavens ! Jameson, Willoughby, White—all our police officers, prisoners, at the mercy of Kruger ! Then a garbled casualty list. Eighty of Jameson's force killed, among them Charlie Coventry and Lindsell ! Other well-known names among the wounded. Deeply and bitterly we cursed the treachery of the Committee at Johannesburg. With dreadful misgivings we wondered whether the Doctor and the other gallant leaders had been shot as conspirators. Our dinner party was forgotten. Most of us broke away at once to seek further news at the Club or the Newspaper Office.

In Bulawayo they got the story in instalments, and when the first news of Jameson's force having crossed the border reached them enthusiasm ran so high that, disregarding distance, they began to organise a force to rush to his assistance ; but when we heard of the affair in Salisbury it was all over " bar the shouting." Indignation meetings were held, of course ; futile resolutions passed ; petitions prepared begging clemency for Jameson and his fellow-raiders and for the intervention of the Home Government. On the scanty information available the population was unanimous in condemning Johannesburg and in applauding Jameson, but we were too far away to count, and could only grind our teeth in impotent despair. Throughout Rhodesia there was a profound mystification. We were unaware of the plot, ignorant of the real circumstances, but unfortunately it was *our* Police that had been deluded into participation in the Raid, and *our* officers that had led them, and in the eyes of the Imperial authorities we were branded as a community of dangerous filibusters who could not be trusted to mind our own affairs and leave our neighbours to mind theirs.

This suspicion clung to Rhodesians for years. In Downing Street I doubt whether, even to-day, it has entirely evaporated. One of the earliest symptoms was the creation of an Imperial watch-dog, styled " Deputy Commissioner," to keep an eye on the Administration, and to command the police and volunteers. The first to fill the post was Sir Richard Martin, a retired Colonel of Dragoons, who might have been a troublesome thorn in the side of the Company, had not the course of events caused him to be relieved of all military responsibility almost as soon as he was appointed, and reduced him to the status of a looker-on. " Whistling Dick," as we called him, in allusion to his principal occupation while in Rhodesia, was a handsome, courteous officer of the old school, who, although he had not seen much service in the field, was a soldier to the finger tips, and deserved to be given a chance to prove his capacity in the native revolt which broke out just before his arrival, instead of being compelled to spend a year doing sentry-go round his own dignity, and writing reports about the Matabele, whom he never set eyes on, except through field-glasses.

In Salisbury and Bulawayo the excitement about the Raid rapidly died down when it became known that the principal officers were not to be shot, but sent home to stand their trial, and when the details of the whole conspiracy came to light. All that concerned us was the vindication of Rhodes and Jameson and our own friends, and we did not care a jot who else might be implicated. I doubt if half a dozen people in the whole Territory took the trouble to read the evidence taken in England before the Parliamentary Committee, or realised the full extent of the political and even international issues which hung in the balance just after the Raid.

I cannot resist telling a story which I had from the lips of the late Mr. Bourchier Hawksley a year or so later. It will be remembered that as Rhodes' solicitor he was called upon to produce to the Select Committee a number of cypher cablegrams which were alleged to have an intimate bearing on the plot to organise revolution in the Transvaal and which had been handed to him for safe custody. He point-blank refused to do so. Suspicion as to the nature of the cablegrams was intensified and it was freely hinted that they contained evidence proving that " Joe (meaning Mr. Joseph Chamberlain) was in it," and that other highly-placed personages were cognisant of what was going on. Great pressure was brought upon Hawksley to induce him to yield. There was some talk of summoning him to the Bar of the House of Commons for contumacy ; of immuring him in the Clock Tower, and of other dire penalties. But he doggedly persisted in his refusal and in the long run nothing was done. The telegrams have been left undisclosed to this day and seem destined to remain a political mystery for ever. After the stress of the enquiry Hawksley was, not unnaturally, run down and was ordered a rest which he elected to take at a quiet village in Switzerland. The only other visitors at his hotel were an elderly English clergyman and his wife, the former of whom, having ascertained his name, asked him one day whether he was related to the Mr. Hawksley who had recently been prominent in connection with the Raid enquiry. Hawksley modestly admitted his identity. " Dear me ! " said the parson, " How very interesting ! And pray, Mr. Hawksley, what *was* in those tleegrams ? I should so much like to see them."

Well, in Rhodesia we soon had troubles nearer home which obliterated all thought of the Raid. First of all, in February, 1896, without warning, the Rinderpest descended upon us. What that meant can only be grasped when it is remembered that the nearest railhead on the Southern route was Mafeking, 500 miles from Bulawayo, and 800 from Salisbury, and that ox-transport was the only means of conveyance for merchandise over the long intervening stretch of road. True, there was a shorter route into Mashonaland by way of Beira and the Pungwe River, but in 1896 the narrow-gauge railway from the river had not reached the Rhodesian frontier, and the difficulty of importing goods through a foreign country with very imperfect port accommodation made this route untrustworthy and precarious.

Within a few days the disease showed itself at a dozen different points ; cattle began to die like flies, and soon the transport roads throughout the whole country were lined with stinking carcases. In the vain attempt to stay the pestilence the authorities prescribed killing—not infected cattle merely, but whole herds where one or two beasts were stricken, including the herds of the Matabele themselves.

Now unknown to the Government and the settlers mischief had been brewing among the Matabele for months. They had not been completely conquered in 1893 and had cherished in secret the hope of rising at a favourable moment and driving the white men back over their borders. Their witch-doctors had been constantly working on their feelings and persuading them that all their troubles were due to the presence of the white men. First they had brought drought, then locusts, and now this mysterious cattle plague. No doubt the news that Jameson and his soldiers (who, as they well knew, were the Matabeleland police) had surrendered to the Boers made a strong impression on them and was used as a trump card by the witch-doctors. But the slaughter of their cattle put the copestone on their mass of grievances and it was this that precipitated the crisis. Towards the end of March they suddenly rose in bloody rebellion, and before the startled settlers had realised the full danger 150 of them had been caught singly or in twos and threes and ruthlessly butchered—in some cases with their wives and little children.

I cannot say anything first-hand about the rebellion in Matabeleland because I was in Mashonaland, and immediately after the outbreak all communication between the two provinces was broken. Nor is it necessary to speak of the way in which the citizens of Bulawayo, Gwelo and other small townships rose to the occasion and organised themselves to grapple with it ; nor of the fighting round Bulawayo and in the Matoppo Hills, and of how hostilities were eventually brought to a conclusion by Rhodes himself, who bravely penetrated into the rebel stronghold and parleyed with the ringleaders. These events have been graphically described by Selous, by Baden-Powell, by Plumer and many others, and quite recently by Mr. J. G. McDonald, who was present at several of the peace *indabas* and has given the world a spirited account of the consummate skill and patience with which Rhodes handled the situation. Had it not been for Rhodes' efforts the clock would have been set back in Matabeleland for years, and the Chartered Company could hardly have survived under the load of debt which the maintenance of an army of troops in the field was piling up.

In Salisbury the news of the outbreak reached us on March the 25th and steps were instantly taken to send a force to the assistance of our friends in Bulawayo and Gwelo. Of course, everyone wanted to go, and there was loud grumbling on the part of the sixty or seventy of the Rhodesia Horse whom the authorities insisted on retaining to safeguard the women and children in Salisbury. Within a couple of weeks a column of 150 men marched off to Matabeleland under Captain Robert Beal, a Pioneer and old frontier Policeman, and took with them about half the rifles and machine-guns in the Company's arsenal and practically all the serviceable horses. With them also went Rhodes, who had only just returned from a flying visit to England to " face the music," and who was moreover barely convalescent from a sharp attack of fever contracted on the journey up by the Pungwe River route.

For two months after the departure of Beal's Column from Salisbury our peace was undisturbed. It never entered our heads that the miserable Mashona tribes could give trouble, and traders, prospectors and farmers remained in the outside districts and went about their jobs in complete unconcern at their isolation among thousands of savages. Then, suddenly, as in Matabeleland, the blow fell.

The first sign that trouble was afoot was given at the Beatrice Reef on the Umfuli River, near the old road to Hartley Hill. There, on the 14th June, a couple of miners were suddenly attacked by villagers from a neighbouring kraal, armed with battle-axes, assegais and knobkerries, and barbarously done to death, together with their native servants. The mutilated body of one of the white men was found long afterwards at the bottom of a well into which the murderers had flung it.

In quick succession similar crimes were reported from all the districts round Salisbury, and within a week of the Beatrice affair 120 white people, including several women, had been bludgeoned, speared and hacked to pieces at lonely farms and trading or mining camps, while many others escaped, God knows how ! In almost every case there were terrible and dramatic circumstances, but I have only space to recount one, which, though typical of many, aroused perhaps greater horror because the victims were so well known and the deed was perpetrated so close to the township.

About fifteen miles south of Salisbury a well-to-do Englishman named Norton had been farming for a year or two at a beautiful spot near the Hunyani River " poort." In April, 1896, he returned from a short visit to England, bringing with him his young wife and infant daughter, together with a Miss Fairweather as nurse-companion, and a farm-pupil by name Talbot. They spent several days in Salisbury buying horses, a waggon or two, farm implements and provisions, and while there engaged two other white men as assistants—Messrs. Alexander and Gravenor. They were thus quite a large party, and their live stock included two magnificent Irish wolf-hounds. Before trekking out they invited my family and myself to spend a few days with them on the farm and get some shooting, and it was arranged that we should drive out on Saturday, the 13th June. When the time came, however, one of my horses was sick, and as no one could lend me a substitute I sent a native runner with a letter postponing the visit to the following week. Two days later, when the disquieting news of the Beatrice murders reached Salisbury, I arranged with the Native department for another messenger to be sent out warning the Nortons, and begging them to come into town ; but this man was never seen or heard of again.

Early on Wednesday morning, the 17th, Norton found to his disgust that all his native servants and farm labourers had

decamped during the night, and he sent Talbot on his bicycle
to Salisbury to report this to the Native department, while he
himself went to make inquiries at the neighbouring village
of Inyamwenda, where most of his boys had been engaged.
It was not a particularly unusual occurrence for Mashona
labourers to abscond, though his suspicions should have been
aroused at their doing so in a body. The other two white
hands were sent out on to the lands to look after the cattle pend-
ing his return with new boys to replace the deserters. So it
came about that Mrs. Norton with her nurse and child were
left alone in the homestead.

What next happened must be based on surmise, though
some evidence was extracted at a later date from native eye-
witnesses. A party of about twenty Mashonas, led by a Matabele, arrived at the house, and, finding the women alone, or
knowing it beforehand, tried to break in. The poor ladies made
a desperate resistance with revolvers, and actually shot several
of their fiendish assailants dead, but were attacked from the
back of the house as well as in front, and were eventually over-
powered. Their dead bodies, with that of the little girl, were
dragged outside on to the veld by the miscreants, who then
proceeded to loot the premises, carrying off all portable goods
of value and smashing up the furniture and everything too
bulky to remove. Simultaneously another party had made
for the lands, where they caught Alexander and Gravenor
separately and killed them both.

Talbot had in the meantime reached Salisbury and delivered
his message, which, taken in conjunction with the Beatrice
murders in the same locality, seemed so suspicious that he was
at once sent back with a mounted police trooper to urge the
whole party to come into town without delay. But, alas!
when they reached the farm just before sunset it was too late.
The homestead had been looted and wrecked. They found a
quantity of spent revolver cartridges on the stoep and in the
dining room, and there were stains and smears of blood on the
furniture. Thoroughly alarmed, they made a hasty search of
the surroundings by the failing light, but could discover no
other trace of the unfortunate family. To stay where they
were was useless, and they made all speed back to Salisbury
with their ominous news. That same night a patrol of police
was sent out under Captain Nesbitt, who discovered in the veld,
a short distance from their home, the battered remains of the
two women. The dead baby was there, too, and the body of
one of the wolf-hounds. The corpses of the two white assistants

were found on the lands the following morning; but although diligent search was made the patrol could obtain no clue to the fate of Norton himself. Weeks afterwards his dead body was discovered at the kraal. He walked straight into a death trap, and was mercifully spared the knowledge of what took place at the farm in his absence.

When the news of this terrible crime, and of half a dozen other murders in the same district, became known in Salisbury, men and women saw red, and were filled with a burning desire for vengeance; but for the moment something more pressing had to be thought of. There were many Europeans in an equally perilous isolation, and at all hazards the attempt must be made to rescue them. Despite the reports now coming in from several quarters that bodies of rebels drunk with blood were closing in on the town, all white men who had horses, and some even who had not, started at once for the neighbouring farms and camps to warn their occupants and help them to rally to Salisbury. Every hour brought tidings of further outrages, and it became apparent that even families living on the outskirts of the straggling township were exposed to grave danger, and must at once be brought to a place of safety. Their own servants, who were mostly local natives, could no longer be trusted, and at any moment a massacre on a hideous scale might take place.

There was only one substantial building of any size in Salisbury—the new brick gaol, which had a central block, comprising a large open ward and about a dozen cells, within a spacious yard. The whole was enclosed by a strong brick wall, about 15 ft. high, on the inner side of which were further rooms. This building was hastily converted into a fort; in the rough quarters which it provided the women and children, to the number of about 200, were unceremoniously huddled, and here they were imprisoned for several weeks. No distinctions were made, and each of the cells, 12 ft. by 10 ft., was used as sleeping quarters for four or five inmates, with such scanty bedding as they could collect in the hurried flight from their homes. One cell was set aside as a hospital, and here in the first week two babies were born. The large ward served as a dormitory by night and a messroom by day, but most preferred to take their meals in the open yard. The usual occupants—the hard-labour prisoners—were allowed their freedom; there was no danger of their attempting to escape! Beyond the encircling wall an outer redoubt of sandbags was thrown up with barbed-wire entanglements, and machine-guns were mounted at the angles. The waggons of such refugees as had trekked in from neighbouring farms were used to form an additional defence. Within a few days an impregnable laager had been constructed, and Salisbury settled down to a state of siege. The men, some 300 in number, were formed into a field force with the squadron of Rhodesia Horse as a nucleus, and all who could be spared from garrison and picket duty were employed as patrols to explore the surrounding districts and to relieve small parties of miners, farmers and missionaries at various outlying camps. There was little hope of saving isolated Europeans, but when the first alarm was given a few such, including even two or three women, managed to elude the bands of rebels and, after incredible hardships, made their way into town.

The relief column despatched two months earlier to Matabeleland had well-nigh exhausted the Company's reserves of horses and rifles, and there was a lamentable shortage in both respects ; but private resources were commandeered, and somehow or other most able-bodied men were equipped with a firearm of some sort, while 30 or 40 mounts could generally be mustered for patrol work. On the summit of the kopje, about a mile from the laager, a signal and observation station was established, to keep the garrison informed by heliograph of the movements of the rebels, but although at dusk parties could often be seen burning and plundering houses and farms on the outskirts of the town, few ventured within range of the rifles and machine-guns in the daytime. On one occasion the lookout post reported a body of the enemy advancing from the further side of the racecourse, but a little later saw that what they had taken to be a party of rebels was in reality only a troop of tsessebe (a kind of antelope). In due course this item of news found its way into one of the Cape Town papers, and was supplemented by an intelligent editorial footnote explaining that " the Tsessebe were a tribe of *friendly natives* residing on the outskirts of Salisbury."

The sudden change from their comfortable homes to the rude and cramped quarters at the gaol was borne with great cheerfulness by the women, practically all of whom were " old campaigners " with previous experience of frontier life. Their feelings of horror and indignation at the dreadful fate of so many of their fellow-settlers were repressed in the desire to render aid to those who were sick or wounded, and gradually the humours of the situation outweighed the privations and discomforts. As the rebels were in possession of the roads and no stores could be obtained from outside, the garrison was reduced

Salisbury Laager

to bread made of a mixture of wheat and mealie meal. The
cattle had all died of rinderpest, and for meat rations we had to
fall back on the time-honoured bully-beef.

Mr. Joseph Vintcent, the Acting Administrator, though
essentially a man of peace, was compelled by the exigencies of
the situation to assume the position of head of the military
organisation. We styled him "Commandant-General," and
even manufactured a uniform for him, the principal feature of
which was a tunic bedizened with crowns and stars and any
amount of blue braid. We called it "Joseph's coat of many
colours," but I don't think he ever wore it.

After three or four weeks had elapsed and the country
immediately round the town and commonage had been cleared
of rebels by the small patrols of volunteers, which kept them
constantly on the move, both men and women began to get tired
of inaction and clamoured to be allowed to return to their
homes. The danger of an attack on Salisbury seemed at an
end, but some of the civilians who had been given the rank
and pay of captain or major rather enjoyed their importance, and would have liked to prolong the state of affairs
indefinitely.

Mr. Joseph Vintcent and the two senior officers of the garrison,
Major MacGlashan, who commanded the Rhodesia Horse, and
Major William Smith, a delightful old character, usually known
as "Mazoe" Smith, who had been elected Commandant of the
burgher force, were all opposed to the breaking up of the laager
until trained troops were actually on the spot. They were
probably justified in this attitude, for their responsibility was a
heavy one, but their caution caused much dissatisfaction,
especially among the women, who began to flout the orders
confining them to barracks, and took every opportunity of
slipping off to their own homes when they could do so unobserved.
Some of them composed a chorus parodied from a popular
music-hall ditty of the day, which they sang with much fervour
at the camp-fire concerts in the evening :—

> "Linger longer laager, linger longer Loo.
> If the laager were no longer, what would Bill Smith do ?
> Mac. will ne'er forsake it, Joe will stay there too.
> Linger longer, linger laager, linger longer Loo."

In the end the "state of siege" was brought to a close by the
simultaneous arrival from Bulawayo on July 16 of the original
Salisbury Column, commanded by Col. Beal, and a squadron
of Matabeleland scouts, under Captain the Hon. Charles White.

But although, with these reinforcements, the local forces were enabled to take the field and the inhabitants of Salisbury to return to their houses, it was unsafe for any but armed parties to go beyond the outskirts of the town, and it was more than a year before the rebels were finally rounded up and normal conditions restored.

CHAPTER XV.

THE STORY OF MAZOE.

A SMALL affair when measured by the numbers engaged, the campaign which was forced upon Rhodesia in '96 was marked by acts of heroism on the part of the settlers which lift it to high rank in the annals of the Empire. It is impossible here to give an account of the many sensational rescues that were effected by small parties of volunteers from Salisbury in the first few days of the native outbreak. There was one episode, however, which, alike for the endurance of those who were cut off and for the bravery of the men who dashed to their succour, stands out by itself in the stirring history of that crisis, and as one who was near at the time, and knew all the actors, I will endeavour to tell the story, which has never yet been recorded in detail.

In June, 1896, the little settlement at Mazoe, 27 miles from Salisbury, consisted of a store and a few huts occupied by district officials, the centre of interest being the Alice Mine, which lay near the end of a valley, eight miles long, skirted by rocky, heavily-timbered slopes on the west and the "Iron Mask" range of hills on the east. Through this valley, and enclosed on both sides by reeds and coarse grass seven or eight feet high, ran the road from Salisbury, and roughly parallel with it was a tributary of the Mazoe river known as the Tatagora Spruit, fed by several watercourses, which formed deep gullies or *dongas* at intervals across the track. A mile or so to the northeast of the mine, but concealed from it by a small hill, were the local telegraph office and the quarters of T. G. Routledge, the clerk-in-charge. At the mine itself there was a comfortable house, occupied by the manager, Mr. J. W. Salthouse, and his young English wife, and close by was the temporary camp of four white contractors, who were busy erecting a battery. A Cape-boy cook and a few Mashona labourers completed the mine staff. The Government officials were the Mining Commissioner, Dickenson, his clerk, Spreckley, and the Native Commissioner, Pollard, but the last-named was absent on duty, and we afterwards learnt that he fell into the hands of a party of rebels who put him to death with revolting cruelty. The only other white man at Mazoe was Burton, the storekeeper, who was ill with fever, but about eight miles to the south was a farm belonging to the Salvation Army, and occupied by Mr. and Mrs. Cass, with whom Mrs. Dickenson was stopping as guest. I have enumerated these white people because they all played a part in the series of poignant events which followed. There were others in the neighbourhood, but with the exception of a Mr. Darling, who was prospecting for gold not far from the mine, they all shared the fate of the unfortunate Pollard.

As in other parts of the country so at Mazoe nothing had occurred up to the middle of June to disturb the peace of mind of any of these good folk. They were leisurely pursuing their normal occupations and occasionally meeting at the Alice Mine, where the Manager and his wife kept open house for all their neighbours. On the 16th Salthouse was informed from Salisbury of the Beatrice murders, and next day he got into touch over the wires with Mr. Vintcent, who urged him to advise the Europeans in the Mazoe district to come into town, and said he would send a waggonette at once to bring in the women. Salthouse lost no time in circulating the advice to all within reach, but Darling was the only one near enough to profit by it. The same afternoon while awaiting the arrival of the promised conveyance, Salthouse, with the help of the men working on the battery, threw up a rough laager on a steep kopje behind the mine, closing it in as best he could with timber and rocks. It was far from being an ideal position, being commanded on three sides by hills and having no water supply, but it was the best they could find near their quarters. Although they did not at once occupy it they took turns at sentry-go, and kept a sharp look out that night, without, however, seeing or hearing anything unusual.

Early next morning (the 18th June) a tented waggonette arrived in charge of J. L. Blakiston, an official of the Telegraph department, who had with him, besides the Cape boy driver (Hendrik), one of the Rhodesia Horse Volunteers, by name Rawson. The transport of the three women (Mrs. Cass and Mrs. Dickenson having in the meantime reached Mazoe) was thus provided for, and towards midday half a dozen of the men started in a party to walk ahead into Salisbury, taking with them some native carriers and a cart with four donkeys to convey their baggage. The ladies got off comfortably about an hour later, accompanied by the sick man Burton, to whom Blakiston gave up his seat in the waggonette. The necessity for all to keep together does not seem to have impressed itself on them, for

Salthouse, who had saddled up his horse, decided that before following he would send off some wires, and for that purpose cantered across to the Telegraph Office. The three remaining white men had been invited by Darling to have a bite of lunch at his camp before starting on their 27-mile tramp, and were walking towards it when they heard the sound of rifle shots from the direction of the Salisbury road. A moment later they were startled at the sight of the waggonette dashing with mules at full gallop round a bend of the road and heading for the mine. Those inside and one man on the tent were firing shots into the long grass, whence answering puffs of smoke were issuing, while here and there black heads could be espied bobbing up and down. Almost simultaneously Darling's party found themselves under fire, and all made a rush for the laager, which they gained in safety just after the waggon, for their assailants' aim was wild and the bullets passed harmlessly over their heads. Salthouse, who had also heard the shots, ran out of the telegraph office and jumped on his horse, but was the last to get home, having to gallop for life through the gauntlet of some hundreds of savages who could be seen advancing on the mine from three directions at once.

Not having expected to re-occupy their makeshift retreat they had omitted to bring in any supplies and there was no time now to secure anything but a *vaatje* (keg) of water which had fortunately been put on the waggonette. The next few breathless minutes were spent by the men—now twelve in number, including the two Cape boys—in arranging a safe shelter for the ladies, and by those who had returned with the waggon in hurriedly relating what had befallen them. It appeared that Dickenson and Cass had kept a hundred yards or so in front of the others until about three miles from Mazoe when those following with the donkey-cart heard shots ahead of them and, pushing forward, saw a number of natives striking something on the ground with knobkerries. One of Dickenson's boys rushed back yelling out that both the white baases had been killed, and on hearing this all the carriers threw down their loads and bolted into the long grass. The remaining four then turned the cart and hastened back to warn the party with the waggonette, but were themselves at once attacked by natives who came swarming down from the ridge skirting the road, and within a few minutes another of their number, Faull, sank back into the cart dead with a bullet through his heart. One of the donkeys was also killed and the rest of the team became obstinate and refused to pull, so the white men, now reduced to three, left the cart in the road and ran towards Mazoe turning at intervals and firing at the oncoming blacks. About a mile from the camp they met the waggonette just as it was approaching a steep *donga* and shouted to the driver, who, seeing that something was amiss, had the good sense to pull up and turn before descending into the hollow. The three then clambered in, the mules were lashed into a gallop, while the men kept up a brisk fire with their Martinis through the open sides and back of the waggon-tent, thereby checking the rebels who were too cowardly to come within closer range than about 500 or 600 yards.

Although they had gained the scant protection of the laager the Mazoe party were in sore straits. They had rifles and ammunition and were protected in some degree against bullets, but they were exposed to the scorching sun beating fiercely on the iron-stone rocks, and had no food nor more than a few pints of water, while round them were hundreds of black devils waiting for a favourable moment to rush the laager and finish them off. Unless relief came soon from Salisbury they had little hope of escape. But how could Salisbury be made aware of their desperate plight ? The telegraph office was over a mile away and the path to it was in full view of the enemy. Yet this was their only hope, and as soon as it was realised the two telegraphists, Blakiston and Routledge, nobly undertook to run the risk and endeavour to send a message for succour. There was only one horse—Salthouse's—and rapidly saddling it they started off from the laager carrying with them the prayers and blessings of the others, who anxiously watched them make their way down the slope and kept up a steady rifle fire in the direction of the rebels in the hope of diverting attention from them. They actually gained the office and managed to send a message which, though incoherent and cut short in the middle—no doubt because they were attacked—was sufficient to apprise headquarters of the gravity of the position. " We are surrounded. Dickenson, Cass, Faull killed. For God's sake——"

For nearly an hour the watchers at the laager saw no sign : then at last the two brave fellows reappeared round the telegraph kopje—one riding, the other running by his side. But the enemy had been watching them too and now worked round to cut off their retreat. First the horse was seen to fall. The rider— probably Blakiston—tried to stagger to the bush on foot but was shot down before he could reach it. The other man gained cover but was hotly pursued by the natives who must have caught him up close to the edge, where both bodies were found some weeks later. To this splendid act of self-sacrifice those who in the end escaped from the Alice Mine undoubtedly owed their lives.

As the afternoon wore on the natives grew bolder and crept forward from rock to rock until they reached the long grass at the foot of the kopje. One gained a position immediately above the laager from which he kept up a steady fire upon its inmates, and several others harassed them from the bush and from some empty huts only 150 yards away. Mercifully their marksmanship was poor and though narrow escapes were numerous no one of the whites was hit. The women behaved with great coolness, and while sheltering behind the meagre cover cheered on the men and kept their bandoliers supplied with cartridges.

Not until darkness came was there any respite and even during the night shots were fired at intervals, showing that the enemy were on the alert. But just before dawn the Cape boy, George, stole out and succeeded in setting fire to two of the huts which had been used by the enemy as cover and in bringing back some biscuits and water from the house. With morning the fusillade recommenced and lasted until after midday, but strange to say, no attempt was made to rush the laager. The natives seemed fearful of coming within range of the rifles and a number of them went off to the store where they spent the morning looting and feasting. They doubtless felt that they had the white men in the hollow of their hand and could take their time about finishing them off.

In Salisbury, distracted as they were on June 18 by the reports of new outrages which were coming in every hour, and from every direction, and which proved that the murder epidemic was spreading like wild-fire through the country, the Company's officials, when they got the unfinished telegram sent by Blakiston and Routledge, felt that at all hazards the white men and women at Mazoe must be saved. A patrol of half-a-dozen volunteers was hurriedly got together and despatched that same evening under Lieut. Dan Judson, of the Rhodesia Horse. After his departure, and therefore without his knowledge, it was arranged that a stronger detachment should follow him as speedily as possible. Judson's party, after some trouble during the night through losing their way in the darkness, reached the Salvation Army Camp in the morning without meeting any opposition, but as soon as they entered the long valley they were attacked by rebels concealed on both sides of the road, and for the rest of the way had to keep up a running fight, halting frequently to fire volleys, and then galloping through the more dangerous parts. Several of the men were slightly wounded, and two of the horses were killed, but their riders jumped up behind others and somehow or other they managed to keep going. Three miles from Mazoe they came upon the wrecked cart lying in the road, with the body of the murdered man Faull lying beside it ; and Judson, fearing that a similar fate had overtaken the whole of the white people at the mine, at first decided to make for the telegraph office and try to get a message through to Salisbury. A little farther on, however, his hopes were raised by hearing the sound of firing ahead, and as they rounded the last bend in the road some of his men espied the laager, upon which at that very moment a fresh attack was developing. Their arrival created a diversion. They pressed their tired horses into a gallop, and charged up the slope under a cross fire, eventually reaching the kopje without further casualties.

Although the besieged party was now strengthened by seven well-armed men, and the danger of being rushed was thereby reduced, the problem of food and water was made more serious, and with the safety of the women to think of, the men were too few in number to risk a sortie in face of the hundreds of rebels who were skulking behind the rocks and waiting for them in the long grass. It was imperative that reinforcements should be summoned from Salisbury. They did not, of course, know that a patrol was already on its way. Tempted by the promise of a heavy reward, the Cape driver, Hendrik, undertook to ride through by night if they would let him take the black horse— one of those that had come out with the patrol—and Judson wrote a letter to Vintcent explaining the critical position they were in, and asking for at least 40 men with a maxim gun and 12 spare horses to be sent at once to their relief. There was nothing panicky about the letter, but even if it had reached its destination its demands could not have been complied with. There were not 60 horses in the whole place, and all available men, beyond the bare minimum retained to protect the laager and its 200 women and children, were engaged on rescue work in other directions. But Hendrik, who started on his plucky errand about midnight, fell in some hours before daybreak with the second party of volunteers, commanded by Captain Randolph Nesbitt, of the Police. Opening the letter, and reading it by the light of lucifer matches, Nesbitt, although he only had 12 men with him and no maxim gun, determined at once to take advantage of the remaining hours of darkness and, with Hendrik as guide, to push on to the Alice Mine. His patrol was unobserved until about a mile from its objective, where it was attacked at close range, but a volley or two sent the rebels flying, and Nesbitt got through with the loss of only one horse, arriving at the laager just before dawn on the 20th.

As senior officer, he took command, and after consulting with Salthouse and Judson, decided that the only chance of safety lay in the bold course of forcing a way through the encircling rebels before they could concentrate. The men at the Alice now numbered 30, and they had 18 horses. Six of these, though unused to harness, were spanned into the waggonette, which Salthouse ingeniously made bulletproof by fixing plates of sheet-iron into the sides and back. The 12 mounted men were divided into three sections, four troopers being sent forward as an advanced guard, the same number detailed as a rear guard, and the remainder kept as protection for the flanks.

The rest of the men had to slog along on foot as escort to the waggonette, in which, as before, the women and the sick man Burton were the only passengers. In this order the party started about noon, but had hardly reached the first dangerous gully (where the women had had such a narrow escape two days before) when they were furiously attacked from the right of the road. Those on foot poured volleys into the grass while the mounted men rode out and cleared the rising ground in front ; but two of Nesbitt's troopers, McGeer and Jacobs, and two horses were shot dead before they got clear of this danger-point. From there onwards for close on 14 miles they had to fight their way, the rebels at some places, where the reeds and grass were thickest, coming up to within 10 yards of the waggon. One of the contractors, Pascoe, with great courage, again mounted to its roof, and from this exposed position was able to advise the others of the whereabouts and movements of the enemy, and thus direct their fire. He also saw that moving about in rear of the rebels, and apparently giving them orders and urging them on, were a number of natives on horseback, and this was confirmed by several of the advanced and rear guards.

Near the Tatagora drift Nesbitt lost another man (van Staaden), killed, and four of the six horses in the waggon. Burton, who in spite of his weakness had descended to take his share of the fighting, received a ghastly bullet wound in the face, and three others were hit. Two of the riders dismounted, and their horses were put into the waggon, which had to struggle along with a team of only four.

What must have been the feelings of the women compelled to sit still and watch at this critical moment, especially the two whose husbands had been foully murdered less than 48

hours before at this very spot ?   Yet neither then nor at any
time during their fearful ordeal did they utter a cry or betray
any sign of terror.   When Burton was hit they helped him into
the waggon and staunched and bandaged his wounds, and
under the hail of bullets rattling on the armour plating they
continually handed out ammunition to the men who were
keeping up the desperate defence outside.   All the latter were
suffering from raging thirst, but dare not stop to quench it
beyond catching up a few mouthfuls of muddy water in their
hats as they helped the waggon through the drift.

How they got past the Tatagora none of the patrol could
afterwards clearly remember, and their accounts were con-
tradictory and confused.   Two of the advanced guard—Arnott
and Hendricks (not the Cape boy of similar name)—lost touch
with those round the waggon, and, as a few miles farther on
Hendricks' horse was found wounded and abandoned, it was
assumed that they had both been killed.   Gamely struggling
on, the main party at last reached Mt. Hampden, 11 miles from
Salisbury, and here, as the ground was open, they could make
more effective use of their rifles.   To their great relief they
perceived that the natives were falling back, and near the Gwibi
River they finally drew off and disappeared.   A short halt was
possible ; the tired horses were watered and fed, and the sorely
harassed fugitives were able to fling themselves down for a rest,
but only for a bare half hour, as the sun was getting low ; they
still had eight miles to travel, and for all they knew further
bodies of rebels might be lying in wait for them.

Just before dark a white man staggered up to the picket
lines at Salisbury supporting a companion, who had a severe
bullet wound through the jaw, upon his horse.   They were
Arnott and Hendricks, who had been cut off during the fighting
near the Tatagora, and finding themselves alone, and feeling
certain that the others had been massacred, had made for the
laager, which they reached more dead than alive.   Their account
of what they had gone through, and their conviction that they
were the only survivors, cast the deepest gloom over the garrison.   A meeting of officers was held, and in the faint hope
that some might have escaped it was decided to try and scrape
together yet another relief party ; but before the hurried preparations for this were complete the sound of cheering was
heard on the north front of the laager.

Slowly out of the darkness emerged the waggonette drawn
by three dead-beat horses.   Peering from the shadow of the tent
could be seen the white drawn faces of the women, too overcome

The Mazoe Refugees

On top of waggon : Pascoe. *Standing on sides of waggon :* Berry, H. Rawson, George (*Cape Boy*).
Back row : Capt. R. Nesbitt, Arnott, A. Nesbitt, Harbord, O. Rawson, Ogilvie, Salthouse,
Fairbairn, Spreckley, Niebuhr, Darling, Coward, Hendricks, Hendrik (*native driver*), and Honey.
Front row : Arnold Edmonds and McGregor (*kneeling*), Mrs. Cass, Mrs. Salthouse, Mrs. Dickenson,
Lieut. Judson (*standing*), H. Pollett (*kneeling*).

to speak and hardly able to convince themselves that the pro-
tracted agony of the past four days was over.   Then on foot
came Nesbitt, Judson, Salthouse and their limping, bandaged,
but undefeated comrades.   Little more than a score in number,
they were all that was left of the inhabitants of Mazoe and of
those that had ridden out 'from Salisbury to their rescue.

CHAPTER XVI.

BACK NUMBERS.

IT is interesting to look back upon the stages by which the opening up of Rhodesia proceeded. First in 1890 came the organised and official occupation by the disciplined Pioneers and Police and a few selected parties of mining men. The following dry season saw a spontaneous invasion on a small scale by a mixed crowd of traders, missionaries, speculators, company promoters; men whose object was big-game hunting, like Lord Randolph Churchill, or scientific research, like Theodore Bent; men with a past and men with a future. Finally, in 1892, a steadier and more permanent class of settler began to appear, together with a few enterprising women, whose presence soon exerted a refining influence on the rough and hand-to-mouth style of living which had become second nature to us. All of these possessed one characteristic in common—a thirst for adventure—and for some years Rhodesia continued to be the Mecca of those Britons of both sexes who avoid the beaten track and strike out new paths for themselves.

This, I think, has had a good deal to do with the shaping of the country's destiny and the distinctive national character of its community. The present generation of colonists, who only the other day rejected the attractive bait of membership of the Union of South Africa, and chose the more onerous task of working out their own salvation as a self-governing state, owe their self-reliance in no small degree to the independent spirit bequeathed to them by the stalwarts of the 'nineties.

Whether by good fortune or good judgment, Rhodes made a happy choice of young men to lay the foundations of the Colony which now bears his name. But the Pioneer expedition, for which he was responsible, was only the first, and perhaps the easiest step. There was a long row to hoe before the work was accomplished, and well it was that there was such sound metal among those that followed and helped through war and rebellion, cattle plagues and famine, to carve out of darkest Africa a new province for the Empire. Thirty-eight years have passed since the occupation of Mashonaland, but a few of those who saw the Union Jack hoisted for the first time at Fort Salisbury in 1890

are still at work in the country. Of the thirty members of
the Legislative Assembly of Southern Rhodesia it is worthy
of note that three were actually members of the Pioneer Corps.
One, Col. Frank Johnson, when only 24 years of age, was its
Commander ; another is Mr. Lionel Cripps, the Speaker of the
House ; and the third is Major Inskipp, the General Manager of
the Chartered Company. The Prime Minister, Mr. H. U. Moffat,
has a connection with the country which began even before the
occupation. His father was for some years British Resident at
Lobengula's kraal, and his grandfather, the celebrated Robert
Moffat, whose daughter married David Livingstone, was the
earliest missionary in Bechuanaland, and the friend and guide
of Lobengula's father. The only lady member of the Rhodesian
Parliament, Mrs. Tawse-Jollie, was, before her marriage, the
widow of the first Administrator of Mashonaland—Archibald
Colquhoun, the Asiatic explorer, who was also a member of
the Mashonaland expedition. So the leaven of the Pioneers is
still working.

Besides those who are still doing their bit in the Colony,
there were many of the original Column who gave their lives
for it in the early wars, and not a few who made their mark later
in other parts of the Empire. At least three of the Pioneers of
Mashonaland became Governors of other British dependencies—
Coryndon of Kenya, Sir Eustace Fiennes of the Seychelles,
and Col. Davidson-Houston of the Windward Islands. Other
names that come to one's mind of those who entered the country
with the Column or immediately in its wake are those of Selous,
the famous hunter ; Robert Williams, the soul of all the mining
enterprise in the Belgian Congo ; Sir Charles Metcalfe, architect,
and George Pauling, builder of most of the 2,500 miles of the
Rhodesian railway system ; George Grey, Henry Wilson Fox,
Sir John Willoughby, Gordon Forbes and a host of others whose
lives, cut short in many cases in their prime, helped to form an
epic seldom surpassed in the records of British enterprise.

Side by side with these were many engaging figures whose
achievements never appeared in " Who's Who " or the Colonial
Office List. It would require the pen of a Mark Twain to do
justice to some of the odd characters who drifted into Rhodesia
in the first six or seven years, attracted there by the chance of
sport, or speculation, or fighting, or all three combined. A
good few of the early arrivals were young men from the Old
Country, who seldom had any more serious reason for seeking
fortune away from their native land than the mischance of
having failed at Sandhurst or run up too many bills at Oxford,

and there was, of course, a substratum of qualified professional men—doctors, lawyers and engineers—who saw the advantage of starting business early in a new field. But there was also a large element of that nondescript and picturesque class of free-lances which in those days was always in evidence when new countries were being opened, but which is becoming rare now that the corners of the world are being filled up.

To this class belonged Digby Willoughby, who was a celebrity long before he sought an outlet for his talents in Bulawayo. A handsome man of debonair appearance and great personal charm, he had spent some years at the capital of Madagascar, where he had attained a high position in the councils of the Queen, who made him a General, and eventually sent him on some diplomatic mission to Europe. For a time he cut a prominent figure in London, and in order to play his part with befitting dignity, he designed for himself a gorgeous uniform which completely put into the shade that of an ordinary Ambassador. He once wore it on some official occasion in Bulawayo, to the utter bedazzlement of his fellow-citizens. What his miliary experience had been no one knew precisely, but as a " General " he could hardly be ignored, and when the Rebellion broke out he was appointed Chief of the Staff, a post which his versatile accomplishments enabled him to fill admirably. He had an enormous fund of anecdotes about his own experiences, and was in great request at social functions ; but when Bulawayo settled down he was out of his element, and after a brief period as an auctioneer he passed out of sight.

Then there was " Curio " Brown, an American citizen, who was sent out to South Africa by the Smithsonian Institute to collect butterflies and anything else he could find, and thought he could best achieve that object by enlisting in the Pioneer force, which was just being formed at the time of his arrival. He went through the usual stages of prospector, farmer and soldier, and found the life so congenial that he became naturalised as a Britisher, and finally entered public life as a member of the Legislative Council and Mayor of Salisbury. How he reconciled these pursuits with his original mission, and whether the Smithsonian collection of lepidoptera was enriched to any extent by his efforts I am unable to say ; but he was a good citizen, and his premature death robbed us of one of our landmarks.

Another delightful personality was the Vicomte Edouard de la Panouse, scion of an old French family, who had served on Marshal McMahon's staff in the Franco-Prussian War, and had spent some years in exploring and elephant-hunting in Mashonaland before the Occupation. When the expedition was starting he induced Rhodes and some of the other financial magnates of Kimberley to put up funds for a gold-prospecting syndicate, and trekked up on the heels of the Pioneers for the purpose of securing mining properties. He took with him his English wife, who, in order to circumvent the regulations against the admission of women, entered the country dressed as a boy—a disguise which deceived nobody. Panouse tried mining and farming with no conspicuous success, and was really more in his element when the rebellion broke out. He joined the defence force as a private, and on the blue fisherman's jersey which was served out to the troops he wore a long row of ribbons, including that of the Legion of Honour. Although an elderly man at the time, he showed great resource and pluck in defending a transport convoy, which he was escorting from Umtali, from the attacks of a large body of rebels, and, though compelled to abandon the waggons, he brought the passengers, including an Englishwoman, safely into Salisbury.

Apart from transport riders, and a few old elephant-hunters like Van Rooyen, Fricky Greef and Hans Lee, who had been allowed by Lobengula to squat in Matabeleland, and were there with their families before the Occupation, comparatively few Boers were to be seen in Rhodesia during the first few years. The Chartered Company were on their guard against the freebooting class, such as those who had shortly before tried to set up independent " Republics " in Southern Bechuanaland, and imposed regulations as to burgher-duty and the shooting of game which discouraged any but the more solid and well-intentioned Dutchmen from entering their territory. Before the Occupation was a year old Commandant Ferreira, a grizzled adventurer who knew the smell of gunpowder before any of us were born, and had fought for the British in the Zulu war, tried, on the strength of an alleged concession from a native chief, to lead a raid of Zoutspansberg Boers into Mashonaland to " jump the Company's claim." But the authorities got wind of their intentions, and Jameson went down to the border with a couple of squadrons of Police and some maxim guns, and induced them to reconsider their plans. Ferreira, finding that bluff was of no avail with the " Doctor," cheerfully abandoned his expedition, and accepted the offer of a billet in the Company's service ; but he found regular duty irksome, and soon returned to the low-veld of the Northern Transvaal.

The " chosen race," on the other hand, was well represented

from the start. Most of those who came up in the pioneer days stuck to the country and did well in it. One of the best known was Ikey Sonnenburg, already mentioned, who was, however, too much of a gambler to amass wealth. His chief asset was a profound knowledge of his fellow-men. Once at Victoria he sat down to a game of Nap in his store with four others, including his own business partner. During the play he had to retire for a minute or so to attend to a customer, and when he resumed the cards had been dealt. The hand he picked up was composed of Ace, King, Queen, Knave and nine of spades—a combination on which 99 men out of 100 would have called " Nap " without a moment's hesitation. Not so Ikey. " Who dealt ? " he enquired. " Your partner," replied some one. " I pass," said Ikey.

An outstanding quality of the Jews was their adaptability. There was one who, having first tried auctioneering and then editing a newspaper without making good, started, on the strength of a half-completed course at some American institution, as a dentist. As long as he confined himself to simple operations of extracting teeth he did quite a fair business ; but his success tempted him to higher professional flights, which proved his undoing. He persuaded a lady to let him take a cast of her mouth with the object of providing her with a set of false teeth. Her husband grew anxious at her long absence, and on calling found the dentist busily engaged, with a sort of cold chisel, in trying to prise out a mass of material resembling concrete in which the poor woman's jaws were firmly embedded.

Before leaving the subject of the early Rhodesian settlers, I take off my hat in remembering the little group of British women who braved the trials of the long trek by waggon, through a country where water was often scarce and the necessaries of life unprocurable, but troublesome insects, reptiles and wild beasts plentiful, to put up with life in ramshackle huts with untrained servants and uncertain food supplies.

Few in number—perhaps not more than twenty or thirty in Salisbury before the Matabele War—the pioneer women of Rhodesia included some outstanding characters. At the head of these I would place Mother M. Patrick, the Superior of the Dominican Nuns of the Sacred Heart, whose devoted work in ministering to the sick, under conditions of extreme discomfort, will never be forgotten by the old hands. The memory of this brave little Irishwoman with the countenance of a Madonna is still cherished affectionately in Salisbury by those who knew her, and is spoken of with reverence by later generations who have only heard of her. Another splendid woman was Mrs. Colenbrander, who spent several years of great hardship, and often of real peril, in the savage surroundings of Lobengula's kraal, where her husband represented the Chartered Company, and of those who became better known in after life I might mention Miss Cynthia Stockley, the talented novelist, who came up to Salisbury about 1893 when a girl in her teens, and is still, I am glad to say, a long way off becoming a " back number."

When we came home for our first holiday we used to hear people say, " How delightful! One continuous picnic! " But there is a wide difference between the picnic as a change from town life and that which one cannot get away from. Fortunately for the country, those women who made Rhodesia their home in the first two or three years following the Occupation possessed the saving qualities of " grit " and a sense of humour, and were able to keep a stiff upper lip in the real crises and to treat the minor drawbacks as " experiences."

CHAPTER XVII.

RHODES.

POSTHUMOUS liberties are taken with the memories of most famous men, and the case of Cecil Rhodes is no exception. One cannot help noticing to-day a tendency, among people who at some time or other crossed his path, to seek vicarious importance by claiming to have worked hand-in-hand with him, to have been the repository of his confidences and to have given him counsel at various critical moments in his career. " Rhodes asked me what I should advise about so-and-so ; " " Rhodes and I decided that the time had come for—something else." These are the sort of statements that are constantly cropping up in conversations and interviews published in the press, and they irresistibly remind one of the paragraphs concocted in the Editorial Offices of Society journals wherein the writers profess to have exclusive opportunities of hob-nobbing with members of the " Upper Ten." In order, therefore, to prevent any misconception as to my own qualifications for recording impressions of Rhodes I had better say at once that although I had many opportunities of seeing him between 1890 and his death, and frequently worked under his direct instructions, he never " consulted " me about a single thing. Moreover, I can only recall being alone with him once, when he gave me a good " dressing down " for hazarding a suggestion regarding Chinese labour, which he disapproved of (but of which I am still unrepentant).

And yet Rhodes was to me, as, I believe, he was to most of those who were in contact with him, in however slight and unimportant a capacity, an inspiration and a " Master." His influence shaped my whole course of life ; I revelled in the idea that I was engaged in his work and felt that for him I would go through fire and water.

At the risk of covering old ground and repeating what has already become familiar by repetition I venture to record my recollections of his personal appearance, his sayings and his mannerisms, of which he had many.

Most of Rhodes' biographers tell us that in early manhood he was of slight, delicate and unimpressive build, but when I first saw him in 1889—he was then thirty-six years of age—he

Cecil Rhodes in 1899

(Standing on the spot where his body now lies)

was a man of robust and commanding physique and of unusually forceful personality. Something about the poise of his head, with its strong jaw and slightly raised chin, proclaimed determination and confidence. No one could have passed him in the street without looking back at him and thinking " What a striking looking man ! "

Closer intercourse betrayed some curious incongruities. From one with such a presence you would have looked for a firm hand-grip ; instead you got a limp touch—hardly a clasp— from two fingers, the other pair being tucked into his palm. From one whose words were always weighty you might have expected a strong, balanced voice. Actually his tones wavered from a bell-like bass to a cracked falsetto—almost a squeak. His eyes were of such a transparent blue as almost to seem watery, but they gazed always straight ahead and after the first glance seemed to look through you to something beyond. This peculiarity was most marked when he was speaking to an audience. He often seemed completely to forget their existence and to be talking to the air. In spite of this his speeches— loosely put together as they were, often rambling, and not always grammatical—commanded rapt attention. His obvious sincerity and belief in what he was saying took possession of those listening and made them feel that he was uttering his very thoughts—almost as though he were talking to himself.

This perhaps explains why proposals which in other men's mouths would have sounded fanciful and even preposterous assumed the character of solid feasible plans when they came from Rhodes. Take, for instance, his speech at a meeting of the Chartered Shareholders in the great hall of Cannon Street Hotel, in November, 1892—the speech in which he revealed his cherished idea of a telegraph line stretching from end to end of the Continent of Africa. Read the passage through in cold print —a verbatim report. It certainly contains nothing upon which a sound prospectus could have been framed. The facts and figures are vague and airy ; the objects set out most unlikely to appeal to sane City men. Yet as unfolded by Rhodes that day with his avowed purpose of saving Uganda, and his half-serious chaff about " dealing with the Mahdi," the project seemed positively to fascinate the shareholders and City men who hung on his words. They saw that Rhodes himself believed in the scheme as a link of Empire and were carried away by his contagious enthusiasm. He got their support, and later on their money, and within a few weeks was at work on the construction of the line itself. It never came anywhere near completion, but the speech had served its object and shamed the Government out of their intention to evacuate Uganda.

Another feature of his public utterances was his habit, when a particular phrase pleased him, of repeating it again and again, turning it over like a child with a new toy. That was his way of emphasizing a point—not a very rhetorical way perhaps, but strangely effective.

Many of Rhodes' minor proposals were far-fetched and unpractical, but attractive at first because of their novelty. He held strongly that religious instruction should form part of the curriculum of schools but wished that all denominations should be placed on an equal footing. He therefore pressed for the introduction into the educational system of Rhodesia of a provision that half-an-hour should be set aside daily in all schools during which the clergy of every denomination should be allowed access to the boys and girls of their particular creed —the Wesleyan Minister to the Wesleyan pupils, the Rabbi to the Jews, the Jesuit priest to the Catholics, and so on. " And if," he added, in speaking of his views, " the father of a particular boy says ' I don't want my son to have religious instruction at school,' that boy must not be allowed to spend the half-hour in the playground. He must have a geography lesson." The plan was adopted but proved unworkable, partly because the Rhodesian schools at that time did not possess accommodation for simultaneous lessons in three or four religions, but mainly because the ministers themselves failed to take advantage of the privilege.

Most of those who knew Rhodes, however casually, were invited to his dinner table, either at Groote Schuur, his Capetown home, or Government House in Bulawayo, or, in a few cases, his farm homestead in the Matoppo Hills, not ten miles from where his body now lies. His parties were never formal or carefully organised beforehand. He never chose his guests for their suitability to one another, or because they belonged to the same set—at any rate not in Bulawayo, where his usual practice was during a morning ride or walk to stop and converse with anybody he knew and ask him up to dinner the same evening. This gave a good deal of trouble to his Secretary, who never knew till the last moment how many to arrange for, but it made the gatherings themselves highly entertaining. Men who hardly knew each other, and certainly had nothing in common, would find themselves neighbours at table, and the parties resembled in miniature the meetings of a Rotary Club.

But Rhodes had the knack of drawing all into the conversation and making them feel mutually attracted by the personal link with himself.

His pleasure in surrounding himself with men of different tastes and professions was evidence of the catholicity of his own nature and suggests a clue to the extraordinary range and variety of the circle of his intimate friends. His character was like the octahedron diamond of the Kimberley mine—a crystal with many facets each reflecting a separate interest—and each interest demanded a corresponding friend or group of friends. Thus, his financial instincts led him to cultivate the society of Alfred Beit, and later of Sir Lewis Michell ; in his Imperial schemes he made a confidante of Jameson ; his enthusiasm for scholarship, philosophy and culture drew him to Rochfort Maguire ; his artistic tendencies to Herbert Baker ; his interest in railway schemes to Sir Charles Metcalfe ; in agriculture to Mr. J. G. McDonald ; his sociability and taste for good living to Captain " Tim " Tyson, and his passion for the veld, for distance and open spaces to John Grimmer. There were many others of varying degrees of intimacy, but these few were typical. It would, of course, be absurd to suppose that there was any such conscious classification or selection in Rhodes' mind. In fact, he would probably have been unable to account for many of his preferences. Grimmer, for example—good-natured to a fault and a fine specimen of a young Colonial, was a stolid, taciturn man, with no special intellectual gifts or business acumen—not at all the sort of person one would have expected Rhodes to pick out for close friendship. It is said that someone once tried to extract from Rhodes what qualities he saw in Grimmer that made him choose him, first as his secretary and afterwards as his constant travelling companion. " You see," replied Rhodes, after a moment's thought, " Grimmer is such a hustler with mules." Certainly between the two there was the understanding of David and Jonathan. I saw a good deal of Grimmer immediately after Rhodes' death, and realised that the world had come to an end for him, and in fact he died, some think of a broken heart, within a few weeks of his patron.

If one tries to discern a common quality possessed by the different types of men whom Rhodes admitted to his intimate friendship, I think it will be seen that in their various ways they were all " doers." He had no use for dilettantes or loafers, and said so with great outspokenness in his last will. But he was keen to appreciate energy in others, and, if their activities could be made to help him with his own programme of life, to get the best out of them. And so Sir Charles Metcalfe, with his ambitious railway schemes ; Sir Lewis Michell, with his methodical business habits ; Grimmer, the " hustler of mules," and a limited number of others all found an armchair in the sanctum of Rhodes' private Rotary Club.

It is probable that he was sometimes imposed upon. That a man should have done something or have something important to say was a sufficient passport to his favour, and where his interest was aroused he failed to see that his society was being cultivated for personal gain. His charity was unbounded and frequently indiscreet. This has been attributed by some to a feeling that by putting a man under an obligation to him he secured his allegiance, but I prefer to think that his lavish generosity arose from a warm-hearted desire to place deserving men on their feet. It is sad to reflect that he was often misled into opening his cheque-book for people who had no claim on him, and were altogether unworthy of his benevolence.

For a man whose plans were thought out so far ahead he appeared to be strangely careless of detail. He laid down broad outlines, and expected the details to be worked out by others to fit in with the general scheme.

It may be supposed that before he began to accumulate his great wealth—when he was struggling first as a claim-holder, and later as a contractor on the Diamond Fields—he must have kept books and attended personally to correspondence, but at the time when he secured the Charter for the British South Africa Company he only dealt with accounts on broad and general lines and seldom wrote letters personally. Subsidiary matters both of organisation and finance he left in the hands of subordinates, one of the most capable and energetic of whom was Rutherfoord Harris—a glutton for work and a man without the slightest fear of responsibility. Whatever opinion may be held of Harris' share in the intrigues which culminated disastrously in the Raid, there can be no doubt that in the preparations for occupying the Northern Territories the main burden rested upon him, and that his zeal and energy were an important factor in making the spade-work of the Charter success.

Although as Prime Minister of the Cape Colony Rhodes had at call the services of an official staff, my recollection is that at this period he had no personal secretary. His private correspondence—such of it, that is, as was not handled by Dr. Harris —was in a deplorable state of muddle, as I once had an opportunity of judging when he sent me from the Charter office to his house in Kimberley to hunt among his papers for some document which he had mislaid. For two days I was searching, and shall never forget the disorder of his shelves and drawers, which were crammed full of letters—some unopened—bills, circulars, receipts and even scrip, without any semblance of docketting or arrangement. As his wealth and generosity were becoming well known it was not surprising that there were a number of begging letters—some from the old country, but most of them from South Africa. One which struck me at the time was from a man in England who, in pleading for a temporary loan, enclosed what he described as his most treasured possession and offered it to Rhodes as a precious gift. It was a post card written and signed by Mr. W. E. Gladstone !

Another singular trait which illustrated Rhodes' disregard of detail was his inattention to the correct spelling of peoples names. Sir Lewis Michell, who, besides being his close friend, was his confidential adviser on finance for many years, and in that capacity must have corresponded frequently with him, told me that Rhodes invariably put a T into his name, making it " Mitchell."

To his own personal appearance Rhodes paid little heed. For the sake of comfort, and certainly not from any such pose as is sometimes affected by men of genius, he adopted an easy, unconventional style of dress—in Rhodesia always a lounge jacket and well-washed white flannels—but there was no slovenliness either in his garments or his habits, and in some ways he set an example to those around him, who in a rough pioneer country were inclined to neglect the refinements of civilized society. He never appeared in shirt-sleeves, for instance, and was most careful, even when travelling or campaigning, to shave early every morning. An unshaven chin in others always irritated him, and often drew a caustic reproof. On the other hand, his thick hair was frequently tousled from a trick he had of running his fingers through it when absorbed in thought or conversation.

He seemed to have no vanities, unless it were a vanity to betray the satisfaction which he derived from the word " Rhodesia." " That country you have named after me," " You have been good enough to perpetuate me for ever," were phrases which fell from his lips more than once in his speeches to the Chartered shareholders, and he made no secret of cherishing the thought that long after he had gone his name would endure in the land which he had reclaimed for the Empire.

He had—or affected to have—a contempt for military display

and etiquette, and entirely failed to grasp the importance attached by soldiers to questions of rank and seniority. It is said that when a dispute arose between two officers during the Matabele rebellion as to which had the right to command a certain relief force, Rhodes, who was accompanying the column, settled the matter by having himself gazetted as its colonel. It was not the first time that he had held the rank, for in Kimberley, some years before, he had accepted the honorary colonelcy of the Diamond Fields Horse, a volunteer regiment chiefly remarkable for the magnificence of its accoutrements. He even consented to be present mounted at a ceremonial parade, and to take the salute, but not in the uniform of the corps, though the loan of one was offered to him. He did not mind the sword, but objected to the sabre-tache, or, as he called it, " that ridiculous filibustering bag."

I have heard his wit described as cynical, but it always seemed to me boyish and straightforward, if slightly ponderous in quality. Having achieved a joke, he was so pleased that he was wont to repeat it again and again. When it became necessary to occupy North-Western Rhodesia, he chose the late Robert Coryndon—at that time his private secretary—to command the expedition and to organise the staff of the future administration. Shortly afterwards he wrote to him for some information as to his progress, and, much to his astonishment, got an answer— not from Coryndon, but from Coryndon's private secretary. This tickled him greatly, and he never tired of telling how he had forfeited the right of direct correspondence with one of his own protégés.

Rhodes was never a great correspondent, and as years passed became less inclined than ever to put pen to paper. When he was obliged to write a note he would scribble a few lines on any scrap of paper with any pen or pencil that came handy. I myself received but one communication from him in his own handwriting.. Having disclaimed any pretence of being one of his personal friends, perhaps I may be forgiven for re- producing this note in facsimile. It was unexpected and related to nothing in particular, but reached me after I had been making some official reports to him during one of his last visits to Bulawayo. I need hardly say that it filled me with pride and encouragement to receive this pat on the back from one whom I had so long regarded with devotion and respect.

Looking back on those interesting times when Rhodes was still with us, certain pictures of him return vividly to my memory.

Sept 1700

My dear Hole

I feel
I would like to write
you that I look upon
you as one of the best
and most loyal servants
the Charter has had the
good fortune to employ

V C J Rhodes

A letter from Rhodes (facsimile).

I see him at Salisbury during his first stay there in 1891, seated on a campstool at dinner in the space between his two waggons, roofed in with a buck-sail.   In front of him enamelled plates and mugs are spread on a bare barrack table, at each corner of which is clamped a carriage lamp.   Captain " Tim " Tyson has prepared with his own hands an appetising stew of buck-meat and tomatoes—the latter a rare delicacy in those days.   Rhodes, in all the flush of first acquaintance with the " land he won," is talking with animation of some relics discovered at Zimbabwe, and proclaiming, with quotations from the Old Testament, his belief that the ancient gold-workers of Mashonaland were Baal worshippers, and that the celebrated conical tower was one of the " high places " at which they sacrificed.

I see him again in '97, playing pool with Lord Grey, Mr. Milton and some of the younger civil servants at George Pauling's roomy house in Salisbury, making prodigious flukes, and chuckling with glee as he picks up our " tickies " from the edge of the table.

Again, in 1898, he is entering the Great Hall at Cannon Street a moment after his re-election as a Chartered Director—not re-habilitation, for through the dark days of the Raid and the Rebellion he has never lost the confidence of the shareholders. Every man of the huge throng in the hall rises and cheers as Rhodes, obviously speaking with emotion, reveals this thoughts : " You get the railway to Tanganyika ; you have sanction for the railway to Uganda ; and then you have Kitchener coming down from Khartoum.   Someone will say : ' Oh, that is one of your imaginative speeches ! '   It is not imaginative.   It is practical. It gives you Africa—the whole of it."

Once more—this time in Bulawayo, in 1900.   Rhodes is sitting on an old leather-covered sofa on the stoep of his house at Bulawayo, earnestly discussing with Colonel Heyman, Bourchier Wrey, and three or four other mine managers the growing shortage of native labour, not thirty yards from the " Indaba tree," where, eight years before, old Lobengula must often have sat brooding with his councillors over the growing menace of the white miners.

Lastly, I see him in the following year at the sanatorium in Kimberley, in rapidly-failing health—a few months, in fact, before the end—with Jameson and his secretary, Jourdan, closely watching him.   He is talking of the railway bridge to be built over the Zambesi, a bridge he will never see in fact, though he can picture it in fancy.   It must go close to the Victoria Falls—so close that the passengers in the train will feel the spray in their faces.

Always he was musing and scheming for some extension of civilisation, some new development which would help his beloved country, and provide more homes for Englishmen, thinking, no doubt, all the time the thought that inspired his last words : " So much to do ! "

He did not survive to see it all done—it is not yet all done, but the work is being carried forward.   " His soul goes marching on."

INDEX